C000301032

MARK HATELEY

Home and Away

MARK HATELEY
Home and Away

with

Tony Francis

STANLEY PAUL
London Melbourne Auckland Johannesburg

First published in 1986 by Stanley Paul & Co. Ltd,
Brookmount House, 62–65 Chandos Place, Covent Garden,
London WC2N 4NW

Century Hutchinson Publishing Group (Australia) Pty Ltd
16–22 Church Street, Hawthorn, Melbourne, Victoria 3122

Century Hutchinson Group (NZ) Ltd
32–34 View Road, PO Box 40–086,
Glenfield, Auckland 10

Century Hutchinson Group (SA) Pty Ltd
PO Box 337, Bergvlei 2012, South Africa

Phototypeset in Linotron, Plantin
by Input Typesetting Ltd, London

Printed and bound in Great Britain by
Anchor Brendon Ltd, Tiptree, Essex

British Library Cataloguing in Publication Data

Hateley, Mark
Mark Hateley : an autobiography.
1. Hateley, Mark 2. Soccer players—England
—Biography
I. Title II. Francis, Tony
796.334′092′4 GV942.7.H/

ISBN 0 09 163870 4

CONTENTS

Photograph Acknowledgements

Thanks are due to Bob Thomas for supplying the majority of photographs reproduced in this book; also to All-Sport, Associated Sport Photography, Colorsport, the *Daily Mirror* and the *Sun* for the remaining photographs.

Introduction

'In the right place at the right time' is one of those football clichés which are hard to avoid. In Mark Hateley's case, it couldn't be more apt. Seldom, if ever, can a footballer say that one goal made him a million, yet that is precisely true of the raw and rampant young centre-forward who was plying his trade in the Second Division one moment, and making his fortune the next. Mark became an overnight sensation after scoring one of England's two goals in a famous victory over Brazil in the Maracana stadium.

Hateley was on that South American tour by chance, but how well he seized his opportunity. Almost before the Brazilian dust had blown from his boots, the twenty-two-year-old son of the swashbuckling Aston Villa, Chelsea and Liverpool striker, Tony Hateley, had been earmarked for a glittering future.

Officials from the Italian club, AC Milan, saw the goal on television and rushed for their cheque books. Instead of worrying about his mortgage, Mark was talking in telephone numbers. As he gathered up his young family and flew them over the Alps, he was mindful of the players who had gone before him: John Charles and Gerry Hitchens for whom the Italian dream turned into a reality; Jimmy Greaves, Denis Law, Joe Baker and, more recently, Luther Blissett, for whom the experience had been a misery.

He needn't have worried. In no time, Mark was a folk hero, mobbed in the streets, dined by the rich and famous, eulogised in the sporting press of this football-crazy nation. And this was a man who, in his own words, 'could have walked through Portsmouth Co-op unnoticed a few weeks ago'. They worshipped him because he scored goals, christened him 'Attila' partly because they couldn't pronounce his name, and partly because they remembered the history books.

Success in the most demanding league in the world bred in Hateley the confidence to make the England number nine shirt his own as Bobby Robson's team set out to qualify for the 1986 World Cup finals in Mexico City. Throughout these hectic and exciting times, Mark kept a personal diary. This is the story of a young man and his family with the world at their feet.

Tony Francis

Foreword

The day that Mark Hateley signed for Milan was a sad one for our leading First Division clubs. They missed one of the best centre-forwards we've seen in the English game for a long time. I saw him develop at Coventry and with the England Under–21 side, where he did so magnificently, and am convinced that he would have matured with Manchester United, Everton, or any of our top half-dozen clubs. It would, however, have taken him longer to do it.

The Italians have something that we in England don't have enough of – time. Time to develop young players, to improve their technique, to build their confidence. In our country we don't have time, we just play! The opportunity to work on the basic skills of the game is lost because of the over-congested fixture list we suffer year after year. What Mark has found at Milan is experts with the patience and the enthusiasm to bring out the best in his game. It has turned him into a much better player in a remarkably short time and there's surely a lesson for us there.

Along with Ray Wilkins and Trevor Francis, he's benefited from having to play in a league which concentrates heavily on defensive play. To outfox that tight-marking system, a player has to sharpen up his wits and his control or perish without trace. If Mark continues to learn as fast as he has so far, he'll be a priceless asset to England not only in the 1986 World Cup, but for many years to come.

He is a classic example of the old-fashioned English centre-forward in the mould of Nat Lofthouse. He leads the line superbly; he's tenacious, fast, brave and bursting with confidence. He fights and chases and loves nothing better than to get into that box when the crosses are coming in. His ability in the air is phenomenal. Don't let me hear anyone say that type of player is out of date in the tactical systems of today. Mark has proved with England and Milan that he's a very special footballer. I doubt there's one Italian club which wouldn't pay a fortune to have him in its ranks.

From a financial point of view, it was a terrific move for him to go to Italy and I have no doubt that it will turn out wonderfully for him. Having said that, I wouldn't like it very much if all my players were on the continent. Keeping a check on Hateley, Wilkins and Francis, as well as the lads based at home, is difficult enough! There's perhaps a tendency for foreign-based players to feel that they're out of sight and out of mind. In the past it might have been true, but there's no need for any of them to fear that with me.

You've got to be a strong person to make a success of it in Italy, probably the most sophisticated league in the world. The riches are enormous, but, as you'll find in this story, the protective, caring warmth of an English club is usually missing. Italian clubs pay fortunes, but it's a more impersonal climate that a player steps into. He's a cog in a well-oiled machine and there's not much room for sentiment.

My advice to Mark would be to keep his feet on the ground and never get complacent about the job facing him. I'm glad he has the strength of a close family around him, and what I want to see him do now is produce his ability season after season like the best of professionals. That's what I loved about Kevin Keegan. He was a fantastic little player; a professional in every sense and a credit to the game. The only reason I could find no place for him in the England set-up was because I couldn't see him playing when the World Cup came along. Events have proved me right, but I would hold him up as an example to Mark and to any other young player hoping to make a name in football. The world is full of people who reached the top and then blew it. Keegan didn't and I don't think Mark will either.

He has everything before him. It's in his hands to become England's centre-forward for the next ten years.

Bobby Robson

1
CHIP OFF THE OLD BLOCK

It's a curious fact that few sons of famous sportsmen grow up to emulate their fathers. One or two have threatened to develop, but found the pace a little too hot – Richard Hutton, Christopher Cowdrey and Clive Allen, to name a few. Mark Hateley is a rarity. From inauspicious beginnings, he has blossomed almost overnight to eclipse the well-publicised exploits of his father. Watching Mark soar above his defender and suspend himself in mid-air is to watch Tony Hateley twenty years earlier. The likeness is uncanny: lanky build; lean face; high cheekbones; shock of dark hair; and that deceptively lazy gait of a goalmouth prowler.

Tony's the first to concede that he was not the world's most sophisticated footballer. Neither was he the clumsy battering-ram his detractors would have us believe. He has carved himself a place in the game's history as one of the most successful old-style centre-forwards of all, and perhaps one of the wealthiest. He was big, brave, strong and deadly in the air. They say he could head a ball harder than most players could kick it! Goalkeepers were constantly deceived by the power of his headers. Because Tony traded in that most treasured of commodities – goals – there was no shortage of clubs prepared to invest big money in his ability.

He became the country's first six-figure footballer when Tommy Docherty paid Aston Villa £100,000 in 1965 to take the goal-scoring phenomenon to Chelsea. It didn't work out. Six goals in twenty-six games was a meagre return by Hateley's standards, but if Chelsea had lost faith in him, others certainly hadn't. No less a judge than Bill Shankly was seduced by his reputation for dispatching the leather into the onion bag with monotonous regularity. So was Brian Clough, who tried to make Hateley his first signing when he took over at Derby County. In the end it was Shankly who bought him for £95,000 the following season despite this warning from Docherty: 'He's terrific in the air, but no good on the ground.'

'Never mind,' replied Shankly, unperturbed, 'they said the same about Douglas Bader!' Hateley repaid the Liverpool manager with twenty-seven league and cup goals as the Merseysiders began to emerge from the shadows as the dominant force in English soccer. Shortly, alas, he was on his way. He'd done the job asked of him at Anfield and found himself heading back to the Midlands where Jimmy Hill's Coventry City was the up-and-coming outfit.

Young Mark, in the meantime, was developing into a fine prospect. During his father's spells at Notts County, Aston Villa and Chelsea, the family home was in Derby where Mark was born on 7 November 1961. The boy soon displayed a passion for sport though, at one time cricket seemed to be gaining a hold. In his early teens in Liverpool, he was approached by the Cheshire league side Ormskirk, who were impressed with his Botham-like ability with bat and ball.

That Mark chose soccer was no great surprise. Tony spent much of his spare time coaching the boy in the family garden and local parks. He says:

> I could always see that Mark had got what it takes, but I had to be very careful not to frighten him off by letting him see that I was preparing him for the future. As far as he was concerned, it was just a case of knocking a ball about with his Dad, nothing serious, but to me it was serious. I said to myself that one day he would make it. At the time, I never missed a school match and became the team 'bus', fetching and carrying the other lads like many fathers have to. The most important thing was to let Mark find out for himself what soccer had to offer.

The fortunes of Hateley senior were a lesson in themselves in the vicissitudes of the game. Thanks to the 5 per cent share players received of the transfer fee, Tony secured his future by moving clubs seven times in twelve years – not that he ever planned it that way. In each case, he was pursued by the buying club without ever asking for a transfer. His nomadic career turned him into one of the wealthiest players of his day and Mark grew up in considerable comfort – large houses in the countryside, more often than not, a Mercedes or a TR7 parked in the drive, and holidays abroad most summers.

However, at the age of thirty-three, Tony's career went into rapid decline. Following a second, very productive spell with Notts County, he moved to Oldham where a knee injury put him out of the game for good in 1974.

Mark was thirteen and those hectic, exciting few years had certainly left their impression upon him, as indeed had the speed with which his father's livelihood disintegrated. If nothing else, the teenager understood the transitory nature of success in the game, and the adaptability it demands of a footballer's family. Mark had lived in Derby, Liverpool, Warwickshire and Nottingham before he reached 'O'-level age. There was the constant problem of moving schools, making new friends and coping with the attention showered upon the son of a famous father who was rarely out of the headlines.

One thing young Hateley did not lack was confidence. In fact, he seemed to his teachers to be over-endowed with it. 'Arrogant' was the adjective which appeared most frequently on his school reports. They wouldn't have realised that it is one quality a footballer requires in abundance if he's to make it to the top. Football, in fact, was a dirty word at school. Time and again, Mark was warned that there was no future in it. That is usually sound advice, considering the tiny proportion of youngsters who graduate to the professional game, but in this case it was wildly misplaced. Fortunately for him, Mark was not a young man to accept advice from people he felt were ill-equipped to dispense it.

Football was in his blood. At the age of thirteen he had a precocious talent recognised, even at those tender years, by George Kessler, the Dutch manager of the famous Belgian club, Anderlecht. By chance the Hateleys were holidaying at the same Majorcan hotel as Kessler, though they didn't know the man. As usual, Mark would find any spare moment to kick a ball around and it was during an improvised game by the swimming pool that he ran rings around a Dutch lad of about the same age. It was Kessler's son, and Kessler, from his sun lounger a few yards away, was struck by the English boy's skills. He introduced himself to Tony Hateley and offered to take Mark back to Belgium where he planned to install him at his own expense in a 'school of excellence' (unheard of in Britain then). Though Kessler was insistent that Mark spend the next five years under tutelage, Tony wasn't prepared to risk it.

The Anderlecht chief wouldn't let the matter rest there, and maintained postal contact with the Hateleys for several months afterwards.

'We were very flattered,' says Tony, 'but at thirteen we didn't think it was a good time to let him go. We hadn't had enough time with him ourselves.'

By then, Mark was already distinguishing himself in local football. He astonished his father by scoring six goals as a twelve-year-old in a Sunday morning charity match between two men's sides. A little later that year, father and son were selected to play in another gala match which included such luminaries as Ian Storey-Moore, the Forest, Manchester Utd and England winger. It's interesting to note that Tony Hateley was withdrawn at half-time while Mark was kept on the field for the entire ninety minutes!

Representative honours were around the corner. In Tony's second spell at Notts County, the family moved from Balsall Common in Warwickshire to Mapperley, a Victorian suburb of Nottingham, where Mark was soon to meet his childhood sweetheart, Beverley Bosworth, the girl he later married. He was chosen for Nottingham schools and forged a friendship with Steve Hodge, a slightly built midfield player who would join Nottingham Forest and Aston Villa and play for the England Under–21 side.

Like Hodge, Hateley was a Forest supporter at the time when Brian Clough and Peter Taylor had been lured to the City ground to restore the club to the First Division. Clough and Taylor's exploits don't need repeating here. When Forest were winning the First Division championship in 1977, they turned their noses up at a tall young centre-forward on their doorstep. Forest eventually exploded the transfer market with the first million-pound signature – Trevor Francis from Birmingham City. Taylor had given Hateley a trial but considered him 'borderline' and not worth engaging.

Mark was waiting for his break. Liverpool and Everton were said to be interested, but Tony counselled against it. His brief spell at Coventry had brought him into contact with Ron Wylie, by now Gordon Milne's right-hand man at Highfield Road. Tony liked the set-up at Coventry and pointed out one very important home truth to his son – Coventry couldn't afford to keep a big first team pool like some of the wealthier clubs, therefore there was a much better chance of a youngster getting his opportunity in the first team. The young Hateley duly joined Coventry with these words from his father ringing in his ears: 'You've got to play in the first team. That's the only place you'll ever learn.'

Mark soon obliged, although he made a mere five first team

appearances in his opening two seasons, and failed to find the net. In his third term, still only nineteen, Hateley achieved the breakthrough, but still hadn't captured the happy knack of scoring goals at the highest level. Nineteen games produced eight strikes, a veritable drought compared with his prolific feats in the reserves where the combination of Hateley and Tommy English was devastating. Coventry were fairly well off for strikers in those days. Apart from English, there was Gary Thompson from the young brigade, all of them trying to dislodge the settled pair of Mick Ferguson and Ian Wallace.

Hateley's best season at Highfield Road was in 1981–2 when he scored fifteen league and cup goals and attracted the attention of the England Under-21 management. For a few years, the Under-21 side had been run by Dave Sexton, with Terry Venables as his assistant. When Sexton became the new manager at Coventry upon Gordon Milne's migration to Leicester City, it augured well for Hateley. Odd then that the new manager, knowing of his prowess as a central striker, should attempt to convert him into an out-and-out left winger. Hateley, nevertheless, has nothing but praise for Sexton – 'a real gentleman and intelligent with it'.

The following season, Hateley scored twelve goals, but felt he was growing stale at a club with limited horizons. Coventry weren't a particularly well-supported club, especially after the collapse of the motor industry and its allied trades in the mid-seventies. They continually had to sell their best players to survive. One by one they trooped away under Hateley's nose: Andy Blair, Gary Gillespie, Garry Bannister, Garry Thompson and others. A team bursting with promise and with an average age of only twenty-one (but for the veteran goalkeeper, Jim Blythe, it would have been even lower) was systematically dismantled and sold. Hateley decided the writing was on the wall:

> It was a good club for a young player to start his career. They didn't care how young you were – if you were good enough, you got your chance. Beyond that, I've nothing good to say about them. They had no ambition. When I saw all the good players leaving, it was obvious that Coventry were a dead-end club. I think they always will be. Getting out was the best thing I did.

If Coventry were short on ambition, Hateley certainly was not. And old family friend, Ken Simcoe, the former Forest and Notts

County striker, recalls a frank discussion with the twenty-year-old while he was still on Coventry's books:

> We sat down for a real heart-to-heart because Mark was stagnating at Coventry. I asked him what he wanted out of life and where he wanted to go. His reply was short and sweet and just about sums him up. He said: 'I want Paul Mariner's jacket.'

Inevitably, the parting of the ways was imminent, though many, Tony Hateley included, saw it as a retrograde step when Mark left Coventry for Portsmouth who'd just been promoted to the Second Division. The club had tradition on its side, but since the days of Jimmy Dickinson it had faded into anonymity in the lower reaches of the league. Mark, however, saw something that no one else seemed to appreciate – that Portsmouth were fired by a driving ambition to emulate their south coast neighbours, Southampton, and carve a permanent niche for themselves in the top flight. No sooner were they back in Division Two than their ambitious manager, Bobby Campbell, set about reinforcing the squad to launch a further promotion challenge which would take the club back to the First Division.

Top of Campbell's shopping list was Mark Hateley. The twenty-one-year-old, thoroughly disenchanted with life at Coventry and apparently overlooked by the big clubs, fell instantly in love with the old city.

> As soon as I first went there, I knew I'd be joining them. I could have stayed in the First Division with Watford or Queen's Park Rangers, even joined Chelsea or Sheffield Wednesday, two of the clubs newly promoted from the Second Division, but Portsmouth was the place for me. I was impressed with everything about the club, right up to the chairman, John Deacon, and, not least, with the town itself. I realised that being in the Second Division could be held against me when it came to playing for England, but, luckily, it didn't work out that way. If you score goals, I don't think it matters too much whether you're in the First or Second. As it turned out, joining Portsmouth was the best day's work I ever did.
>
> Everything was positive. Even though I'd spoken to

> John Neal at Chelsea the same day, I automatically wanted to join Portsmouth. With players like Alan Knight in goal, Alan Biley up front, and Kevin Dillon, a player in Glenn Hoddle's class, it seemed to me that they were going places. It was only a matter of time.

The Hateleys – Mark, Beverley and their young daughter, Emma, moved to the south coast for what they imagined would be a long stay. Lucy was born in Chichester hospital shortly afterwards. They bought a lovely four-bedroomed house near Hayling Island, inhaled the warm sea air and thought the good times had arrived. Mark signed a three-year contract at £25,000 a year.

Already the relationship with his father had grown more distant. Tony Hateley had tried various business ventures in the north-west and settled down to become sales manager of a local brewery. Geography alone dictated that father and son would see less of each other. Over the years, Mark had spent more time at the home of his in-laws in Nottingham than with his own parents who were now divorced.

His father-in-law, Charlie Bosworth, a car dealer and building speculator, had become his confidant. Although Mark says he telephoned his father twice about leaving Coventry for Portsmouth, Hateley senior was hurt:

> I didn't know anything about the Portsmouth move until it was all over. I was very disappointed that Mark hadn't taken me into his confidence, and worried that he'd joined a Second Division club. It seemed a step backwards to me.

A step backwards it certainly was not. Though Portsmouth missed Campbell's dream of immediate elevation to Division One and finished half-way up the table, Hateley had a wonderful season, scoring twenty-five goals in the league and cup and making a dramatic impact on the England Under-21 side which won the UEFA tournament for Under-21 teams. The competition was spread over two years between 1982–4 and it had been far from certain that Hateley would play in the closing stages:

> To be honest, I thought my chance had gone when I was sent off in the match against Scotland in 1982. That gave me a four-match suspension which ruled me out of

the build-up to the quarter-finals. After the suspension I missed one more game, then, to my surprise, I was called back into the side during my first season at Portsmouth. I had a poor game at Newcastle against Hungary and was eventually pulled off.

The next game was the quarter-final against France at Hillsborough, and everything just clicked into place.

England beat France 6–1 with Hateley scoring four and further goals coming from Dave Watson, the Norwich central defender, and Sheffield Wednesday's exciting young fullback, Mel Sterland, playing on his home ground. The return leg went just as well, Hateley heading the only goal of the match at Rouen.

Now, only Italy stood between Dave Sexton's young team and the final. Club commitments forced Hateley to miss the first leg at Maine Road, Manchester, where England took a convincing 3–1 lead. Mark Chamberlain, the black winger from Stoke, put England ahead, Mich D'Avray of Ipswich scored the second, and Sterland completed the victory from the penalty spot. A 1–0 defeat in Florence failed to stop England progressing to a two-leg final against Spain. In that match in Florence, Hateley came up against the young Italian defender, Fillipo Galli, who was soon to be his new team-mate.

The trophy was firmly in England's grasp after another Sterland goal gave them a precious 1–0 lead from the away leg in Seville.

In May 1984 things were about to change for Hateley. He couldn't have known at the time, but a dizzying sequence of events was about to catapult him from comparative obscurity to international stardom within a few short months. It began with the return leg of the Under–21 final at Bramall Lane. England beat Spain 2–0 to retain the UEFA trophy they'd won in 1982. Hateley scored the goal which sent England on their way, that balmy Wednesday evening. Up in the stand, watching closely, was Bobby Robson, manager of the full England side.

He told Hateley to get himself to Scotland the following Saturday because he was considering giving the raw young striker his first senior outing, against Scotland at Hampden Park. Mark drove from Portsmouth to Glasgow with his father-in-law in a state of high excitement. In the event, Robson didn't play him, but it was at least a taste of full international football and Hateley felt it had been good to show his face.

The English season was over. It had been Hateley's best so far. If he thought he was due for a rest, he had another think coming.

Bev and I were just planning to take a family holiday when I got word that I could be included in the party for England's summer tour of South America. Sure enough I got the nod and the entire squad was called together for Keith Burkinshaw's testimonial at White Hart Lane.

That game scuppered the touring chances of another fine young striker who was clearly vying with Hateley for one of the front-running positions. Gary Lineker of Leicester City tore a groin muscle and withdrew from the South America trip. As luck would have it the resident central striker, Paul Mariner, was already ruled out through injury and Trevor Francis was committed to playing for Sampdoria in the Italian Cup.

It was a series of fortunate circumstances. When the party left for Brazil, I was the only genuine centre-forward in it. Robson had already indicated that he planned to use a central striker supported by two wide men, Chamberlain and John Barnes. It didn't need an Einstein to work out that my big chance was about to come.

Before the trip I'd had a ten-minute outing for England at Wembley against Russia, coming on as substitute late in the game. I was disappointed not to have been given more of a game, but delighted when the manager took me aside and said: 'Paul Mariner's been a great servant, but it's you I'm looking to for the next ten years.' There was no point in getting carried away. I knew that if I didn't produce the goods, I wouldn't keep my place for two weeks, let alone ten years!

With that, Hateley, still only twenty-two, reported to Heathrow Airport in June 1984 for his first visit to South America. England would play three friendly internationals against Brazil, Uruguay and Chile as part of Robson's early preparations for the Mexico World Cup two years ahead. First stop was Rio de Janeiro.

Hateley was still in nappies when Pele, Didi and Vava won the 1962 World Cup in Santiago, a school infant when Geoff Hurst's hat-trick demolished West Germany four years later, and a television soccer addict by the time Pele again, in the company of Jairzinho,

Gerson and Carlos Alberto, dismembered Italy 4–1 in the Aztec stadium, Mexico, in 1970.

Bobby Robson was as good as his word. Hateley was picked to play up front with Woodcock, Chamberlain and Barnes for the Brazil game, a game which was to alter the direction of his career. Rio's magnificent Maracana stadium was a shop window to the world.

> What a place to make your full debut. Rio was fantastic – mountains, beaches, ocean and streets packed with singing, dancing people.
>
> The spirit of the England squad was marvellous. We did everything together, eating, sightseeing, relaxing. It was a fantastic, stimulating atmosphere. I roomed with Gary Stevens, my old pal from the Under–21 team, but the camaraderie was so good that you could have happily roomed with anyone. I can't remember much about the match because it seemed to flash by.

Few others will forget England's performance that day. Although Brazil were without three of their finest players, Socrates, Zico and Falcao, they still fielded a formidable side including Junior, the young pretender who would soon find himself in the Italian League with Torino. England threw caution to the wind and played the world masters at their own attacking game. The result was a 2–0 victory and a welcome tonic for the English game. It will be best remembered for a quite stunning solo goal from Barnes who, black limbs swaying past defender after defender, could have been a Brazilian himself. But it was a reaction goal from Hateley which was being noted in one particular corner of Europe – that and his prodigious ability in the air.

Ever since John Charles terrorised defences with his aerial assaults for Juventus in the late fifties and early sixties, the Italians have been in awe of British centre-forwards. In 1963, Juventus had fleetingly considered Tony Hateley as a replacement for the ageing Charles, but despite intense speculation that the Aston Villa striker was destined for Turin, no official inquiry was ever made. Twenty years later, his son's England debut had sent a shiver of anticipation through the Via Turrati, famous headquarters of AC Milan.

The England-Brazil game was shown live in Italy. Part of the captive television audience that afternoon was Guiseppe Farina, the Milan president. He'd been more interested in the Brazilian, Renato, but received this call from a scout who'd been detailed to report on Renato. 'Never mind Renato. What about that English centre-forward, Hateley? He's a sensation.'

That same evening, another telephone was ringing south of the Thames. The caller was Gino Santin, a rich restaurateur in Ealing who was under contract to Milan to supply information on English players and act as interpreter when the deals were being struck. Like so many British-based Italians, Santin was football potty. He'd think nothing of travelling to Milan just to watch his team play. Money was no real object – his family had virtually owned the Adriatic resort of Lido di Jesolo and made a fortune selling the land to package tour operators and hotel builders.

Santin had been watching television too. When his call was answered, he enthused endlessly about Hateley and swore that this was the man Milan were looking for. At the other end of the line Ron Noades, the Crystal Palace chairman, permitted himself a small sigh before reminding his good friend Santin that Hateley was the player he (Noades) had recommended several weeks earlier. At the time, neither Santin nor anyone else had shown the remotest interest. They'd never heard of Hateley.

Almost overnight, Hateley's name was on everyone's lips. Noades set to work arranging meetings between Milan's general manager, Antonio Cardillo, and Portsmouth's millionaire chairman, John Deacon. One's entitled to ask why the chairman of Crystal Palace was acting as go-between? It's a question the Football League would love to have answered, though there's nothing in the regulations to forbid the practice. The League's view is that while the involvement of a chairman in the affairs of another club isn't exactly desirable, there's nothing they can do about it. Under FA and FIFA rules, it's forbidden for anyone to establish a brokerage for transfers based on a percentage take, but when it comes to scouting for overseas clubs, even setting up the deal, there seems to be no restriction. Noades, the man who helped to revive Wimbledon before buying Palace, was possibly the single most important influence in the Hateley transfer. *He* certainly believes so.

Noades's Italian contacts were founded in the mid-seventies when he took youth teams to Jesolo for international tournaments. That's where the Santin connection comes in. Over a period of time, the two became close friends and Noades was later to build two restaurants and a wine bar in London for Santin. Their mutual love of soccer led to Noades's involvement with Milan. In his words, he became their 'man on the ground' in England, passing information to Milan via Santin about worthwhile investments from the English and Scottish leagues.

Apart from Hateley, Noades claims to have engineered the transfer of Wilkins to Milan. On his advice, Milan had seemingly been eyeing Gordon Strachan, the little Aberdeen striker. Our 'man on the ground' says he persuaded the Manchester United chairman, Martin Edwards, that he'd be better buying Strachan before Milan made a move, then recouping his money (and more) by selling Wilkins to Milan instead. United *did* buy Strachan, for £600,000 – and collected £1.5m from Milan for Wilkins. Noades swears he's never accepted a penny for his trouble and insists: 'My conscience is clear.'

Milan were almost frantic for a new striker. In Italy, transfer negotiations are publicised quite openly in the newspapers. Most major towns support a daily sports paper, and in order to fill the column inches it seems that every cough and hiccup from the boardroom is reported. The fans are whipped up into a frenzy by gossip, by speculation over new deals, and by the opinions of everyone in football about everything that moves. If Milan didn't come up with the goods soon, the *Tifosi Rossoneri* (red-and-blacks supporters) would cancel season tickets, boycott the stadium – anything was possible.

To make matters worse, the Italian deadline was fast approaching. Attempts to sign Renato, Gomes from Benfica, or Rudy Voeller of Bayern Munich had all bitten the dust. The man they really wanted (as did half of Europe) was Liverpool's Welsh striker, Ian Rush, who'd just hit forty-six goals in the 1983–4 season. Time and again Milan's overtures were rejected. Still Cardillo and Farina clung to the vague hope that money would change his mind. It didn't, of course, and that's when the desperate message went out to Noades: 'Find us an old-fashioned striker quickly!'

Noades came up with Hateley and Mick Harford, the Birmingham striker who would shortly move to Luton. No reaction. The England-Brazil game came just in time. Noades was vindicated. Cardillo immediately sent word to Ray Wilkins in South America. Wilkins was in the England party with Hateley, having recently completed his career with Manchester United. He was 'sold' to Milan for £1.5m three months earlier but still saw out his contract at Old Trafford.

It was the bilingual Santin who spoke to Wilkins. What did he make of Hateley? Wilkins was enthusiastic but cautious:

He'll be England's centre-forward for the next World Cup if all goes well. He's terrific in the air and has better technique on the ground than most. The only problem: he's very young.

Cardillo didn't want to hear any more. Milan's new coach, Nils Liedholm, poached from Roma whom he had guided to the Italian championship and the European Cup final, gave his full backing to the Hateley lobby. He recognised in the raw young Englishman the same qualities he himself displayed as a centre-forward with Sweden in the fifties. Curiously, Liedholm too had had the nerve to score against Brazil . . . in the 1958 World Cup final in Stockholm.

Things were moving fast now. Noades arranged the summit between Portsmouth and Milan, and Cardillo was swiftly on his way to England.

2
AN OFFER HE COULDN'T REFUSE

As usual in these cases, the last person to be aware of developments was the player. Hateley felt confident that his arrival on the international scene would alert the interest of clubs like Liverpool, Spurs and Manchester United, but hadn't given a thought to playing on the continent.

> Out of the blue, Ray told me he'd had a phone call from Milan and asked me how I'd fancy playing in Italy next season. I thought he was joking. Me, a Second Division player who'd still to fulfil two years of a three-year contract at Portsmouth? Ray explained that they'd seen the Brazil game on television and were keen to sign me. I was thrilled, but said I'd wait and see what developed.

What developed was the move of a lifetime. From a basic £25,000 a year at Portsmouth, Hateley leapt into the supertax bracket. His three years at Milan would net him a quarter of a million pounds basic salary with a guaranteed minimum win bonus of £25,000 a year, and huge incentives for winning the championship or the Italian Cup or qualifying for Europe.

It was fortunate for Hateley and for Dennis Roach that the player had recently decided to take on an agent. Roach, a St Albans furniture dealer, had made his name running the affairs of Johan Cruyff (after a chance meeting on a Mediterranean beach), advising and negotiating three £1m transfer deals for Trevor Francis – to Nottingham Forest, to Manchester City, to Sampdoria. The bulk of his business was arranging trips and competitions abroad for clubs all over Europe and he's one of the few agents with a UEFA licence. Roach's dealings had brought him into contact with Bobby Campbell, Hateley's manager at Portsmouth, who advised the player to seek professional guidance once he became involved in the England set-up. Campbell apparently suggested Roach.

Reports of the subsequent transfer dealings vary somewhat. Noades says it was *he* who arranged the meeting between Deacon and Cardillo in an Italian restaurant off London's Savile Row. He insists that he and the Italian delegation were surprised to see Roach turn up, and that Santin was ordered to make it clear to Hateley's agent that Milan didn't want him involved. Roach had in fact been invited by Deacon to safeguard Portsmouth's interests. The Pompey chairman had no experience of transfers to Italy and requested Roach's advice. Then a funny thing happened. Once it became clear that Milan wanted no dealings with agents, Deacon feigned surprise at Roach's presence and simply dropped him.

In any case, Roach had wanted no part in the discussions and only attended, along with his solicitor, Peter Baines, as a favour. His only business was to act as advisor to Hateley in the tricky contract negotiations with Milan.

The clubs at any rate agreed on a fee of just over £1m. The contract was signed at a Hyde Park hotel at one o'clock the following morning, with Portsmouth showing a handsome profit of £800,000 on a player they'd bought a year earlier.

Roach's main business was to come, helping Hateley to negotiate his contract with a group of businessmen as sharp as any in the football world. The rendezvous was fixed for Santin's luxury residence at Denham, a stone's throw from Heathrow airport. Noades took no part in the meeting and Roach was aware that Milan simply used Santin as an interpreter, nothing more. The delegates that sunny June morning were Roach, Hateley, Baines and Charlie Bosworth on one side; Cardillo, Silvano Ramaccioni (one of the Milan directors), and Ron Teeman (a Leeds-based lawyer) on the other. For the moment, Deacon and the Portsmouth secretary Bill Davis sunned themselves in Santin's garden while Roach 'went to war' with Cardillo and Santin did his best to interpret.

Serious though it was, Hateley couldn't help being amused:

> The Italians were jumping up and down waving their arms about, just like a scene from *The Godfather*. The air was thick with smoke. No sooner did they light up

> a cigarette than they were putting it out and lighting another one. Papers were flying in the air. It was all very dramatic.

Throughout this frenetic kindling and re-kindling of cigarettes, the Italian contingent was bargaining hard. They knew Hateley wanted to join Milan and traded on that and his inexperience. Roach would have none of it. He acknowledged that Hateley had only three international appearances behind him and that he wasn't an established figure like Francis or Graeme Souness. Nevertheless, Roach had one ace up his sleeve: the Italian transfer deadline closed at midnight that very night, 27 June, and Milan were desperate to pull off a second major signing to appease supporters who were growing more than a little weary of promises.

Cardillo talked of a West German and a Portuguese alternative if Hateley didn't like the terms, but Roach had a shrewd idea they were bluffing. What he possibly didn't know is that in the meantime, Milan were making a last effort to spirit Ian Rush away from Liverpool. However, the player showed marked reluctance to leave Anfield and told Milan that if he *did* leave, it would be for one of the glamour clubs like Juventus or Roma. It gradually became clear to the Hateley delegation that there *was* no alternative. As the clock ticked on and the dirty teacups piled up, Roach made his demands plain. He wanted his client to have a three-year contract which would ensure him a substantial sum in the bank at the end of the day and enable him to live comfortably in a country where the living expenses were high. The smiles disappeared and the bargaining became brusquer, for it appeared that Roach had pitched too high. Suddenly, Hateley's agent called the negotiations to a halt.

> Their terms were completely unsatisfactory. I knew because I'd advised Trevor Francis when he went to Sampdoria, and Ruud Krol when he was transferred to Naples. What's more, I knew Falcao was on £72,000 a month at Roma. What Milan were offering Mark was peanuts by comparison. Admittedly they were taking a risk on a relatively unknown quantity but that was no reason to deny him a decent wage. If there was to be a repeat of the Luther Blissett fiasco, I didn't want my client suffering financially like Luther did. He's still

reportedly owed a lot of money by Milan which he'll be lucky to receive.

Roach swung his heavy six-foot-three frame out of the conference room and went back into Santin's lounge where Hateley and Charlie were waiting. He told them: 'The deal's off but sit still for five minutes, there's no way I'll let them drive away.'

He needn't have worried. Within three minutes, Teeman the lawyer opened the door to the lounge and told Roach to work out a compromise package. It was 2.30 p.m. and discussions had been in progress for almost four hours. Cardillo was up against it. At 4 p.m. his flight left Heathrow and if he didn't lodge the documents at the Italian League office in Milan by 8 p.m. they ran the risk of missing their man. With pens scratching furiously, a mutually satisfactory document was drawn up and signed in less than 180 seconds. Cardillo and Ramaccioni sped away to the airport, praying that the flight wouldn't be late.

Hateley gave a cursory glance to the agreement and wondered if he was dreaming. It promised a potential half-million in three years and that was only the start. Roach's principle is that a player should live off his bonus and bank his wages. There'd also be a house with the job, a car, a prescribed number of free flights to and from England during the year, and free medicine and schooling for Hateley's two daughters. It was, as Roach proudly pointed out, 'A family package designed to make sure that not only was the player happy, but his wife and children would have every convenience to make settling in a foreign land as comfortable as possible.' Quite rightly, he'd persuaded Milan that it was in their interests for Hateley to be settled and happy. It was the sort of deal which might well have avoided many of Blissett's problems the previous season. But Blissett didn't have an agent to work it out for him. His contract was negotiated by Watford who may well have seen the Milan adventure as a way for Blissett and themselves to make a quick killing before teaming up again in the future. The deal had been masterminded by Noades but seemed doomed to failure from the start.

Like Hateley, Blissett was a third choice. At the end of the 1982–3 season, Milan were anxious to sign Rush. When it quickly became obvious that Rush wasn't interested, the Italians switched their attention to Norman Whiteside, the teenage striker who'd been the youngest player ever to pull on the famous red shirt of Manchester United. Noades did his best to persuade United and Whiteside that he should move to Milan for £1.5m but the message from Whiteside, who was holidaying in the USA, was negative. He was still in love with Manchester United and that was that.

In almost identical circumstances to 1984, Milan had been faced with a minor crisis: the transfer deadline was nearly upon them and they had to deliver the £1m striker the fans had been promised for the new season. Cardillo and his men did no more than look at the top goal-scorers list for the English League and decide that Luther Blissett was their man. Noades says he warned Milan that Blissett wasn't their type of player, but it was no use. Cardillo had made up his mind without even seeing the Watford striker, and apparently without even realising that Blissett was black. Black footballers, indeed blacks of any persuasion, are a rare sight in Italy, so Blissett was bound to attract unwanted attention.

It didn't seem to matter to Milan. Nor did the fact that Watford would have settled for £600,000. The Italians had to present a £1m player to their supporters and insisted on paying £400,000 more than they need have. Such is the nature of Italian football.

The move, naturally enough, was a disaster. Blissett was a fish out of water. Away from the cosy familiarity of Vicarage Road, he couldn't cope. There was no Graham Taylor to put a comforting hand on his shoulder, no business advisor to step through the minefield of his contractual obligations, and no family to provide moral support. Unlike Hateley and Wilkins, too, Blissett had no other Briton within sight. He was well and truly alone. Add to that the fact that he was miscast as an old-fashioned centre-forward (something he most decidedly wasn't) and you have the recipe for serious trouble. The best that can be said is that he toughed it out, playing all thirty matches in the Italian League, but managing only five goals.

Two seasons before, Milan had splashed out £1m on the Manchester United striker, Joe Jordan. Their predilection for an old-fashioned centre-forward was already becoming an obsession. Jordan was probably past his best, as anyone in Britain could have told the Milanese director. The Scotsman's first season with them was catastrophic. He scored two goals and the club was relegated to Division Two. To be fair to Jordan, he *did* score ten goals in helping Milan to climb straight back into the First Division the following season, and went on to help sow the seeds of future success at unfancied Verona. Nevertheless, recent history was not on Hateley's side and it is greatly to his credit that he never let it distract or disturb him. Hateley, as will become apparent, is an unusual young man, confident, sensible, determined, and thoroughly unflappable.

If he didn't realise at the time of signing, the fertile minds of the Italian press would soon remind him of the most preposterous flirtation Milan ever made with an English footballer. Hateley was still a few months away from first seeing the daylight when Jimmy Greaves began his brief and tragic career with AC Milan. The word 'tragic' is not a casual overstatement. As Greaves confesses in his autobiography:

> I can pinpoint the day, the hour, the minute, the second that I doomed myself to life as an alcoholic. It was the moment I signed my name on a contract which tied me head and foot to AC Milan . . . Over a period of about a year, I was in a state of turmoil. Frightened, frustrated, bored, aggravated, depressed. All the classic ingredients that drive a man to drink.

It was 1961 and the Italians had lifted their embargo on foreign players. In England, footballers toiled for a maximum wage of £20 a week, although Jimmy Hill was about to blow the whole wage structure apart. Greaves didn't know that when he signed from Chelsea for £80,000. It's not hard to imagine the attraction of Italy. It would have taken Greaves ten years in the Football League to earn the £10,000 Milan were offering as a basic three-year wage. In addition to that, he would receive at least £5,000 in bonuses.

As we know, the transfer backfired dreadfully. Despite becoming top scorer with nine goals in fourteen games, Greaves stayed only half a season in Milan before 'escaping' from his Italian 'prison' to join Spurs. The Italian press crucified him; the English press was moved to call him 'a spoiled little brat' and Greaves was, as he says, well on his way to a life of alcoholism with all its attendant misery. A quarter of a century later, Jimmy has conquered new peaks as a television pundit and taken more than a passing interest in the adventures of Mark Hateley:

> I think it's been a good move for Hateley. He has the chance to set himself up for life, and I wish him the very best of luck. If the same opportunity had presented itself to me in this day and age, I would have to be tempted. The world has changed a lot in the last twenty-four years. It's a much smaller place and the Italians and the English understand each other better. After all, people *commute* to and from Milan today. When I was there, you

could only get two flights a week to and from England – and I kept missing them! The majority of folk hadn't even dreamed of a holiday in Italy. There was no such thing as a package tour.

If I'd stayed, I could have been a very rich man, but don't forget, it wasn't only me failing to make a 'go' of it. Dennis Law and Joe Baker had each other for company at Torino and they couldn't stand it either!

When all's said and done, though, I'm not convinced it's right that British players should go abroad. I tell Bryan Robson and Glenn Hoddle I'm delighted that they're still here. Our football can't afford to lose players like that and it would delight me if the drain of talent dried up. After the UEFA ban on English clubs in Europe, it must be doubly tempting for anyone to go to Italy, Spain or Germany, but I've a feeling that the ban won't last very long. The world knows now that it wasn't just Liverpool fans at fault in Brussels – the Belgian authorities had made a terrible mess of the arrangements at the Heysel stadium. We couldn't say so at the time, but we know it now.

Whatever they say about the skill factor in the Italian League, I still believe that our league is the best in the world. I know we see our fair share of drab games, but against that, we see some terrific action as well. What's unreasonable is the way we've tried to pay footballers the moon when the English game couldn't afford it. There was never any economic sense to it all. In Italy, it's a different story. The supporters are prepared to pay much more for the privilege of watching and teams like Milan, who offer huge contracts to players, attract full houses every home game. For that reason, I expect the big money deals will continue.

I'm pleased to see that Hateley has a trainer who gets on with him. When I was there, we had a bull of a man called Rocco who disliked Englishmen, and wasn't afraid of saying so – frequently. For his own good, I feel Hateley will have to watch himself out there. He's an aggressive type of player and we all know how murderous those Italian defences can be. Ray Wilkins can carry on

in midfield until he falls asleep with old age, but it's an entirely different business being a striker. Hateley can give a bit of stick, but judging by some of his injury problems in Italy, he's going to get a fair old pounding.

So Hateley was on his way to Milan with the blessing of Nils Liedholm. The very day that he signed, Liedholm was bidding Roma goodbye with victory over Verona in the Italian cup final. Hateley meanwhile had decided to fly to Italy within hours of concluding the transfer. He took with him the lawyer, Baines, and, coincidentally, found himself on the same flight to Linate as Cardillo and Ramaccioni. They'd missed their four o'clock departure, but were still confident they could beat the deadline for foreign players.

During their enforced delay at Heathrow, the Italian party had sent word that Hateley was now a Milan player. The message spread like a bushfire across that part of northern Italy, and even as Hateley boarded the plane an impromptu reception was taking shape.

3
IN TERRA ITALIANA

Wednesday, 27 June – Thursday, 28 June

Hundreds of fans were waiting to greet us when we stepped off the plane. I'd never seen anything like it. Couldn't believe they were there for me. Word must have got around fast. For a player coming from England it was staggering. When I was with Coventry we'd have been flattered to get that many fans travelling to an away match! The club put us up in the Principe di Savoia hotel, one of the smartest places in town. I was impressed. It was the red carpet treatment all the way. Vice-president Gianni Nardi came to collect us in his BMW and took us to one of the city's top restaurants to meet the Milan chairman, Guiseppe Farina.

He's a big man with hands like shovels. They tell me he farms vast acres in Italy and South Africa. It certainly looks as though he was raised on the land. Seafood truffles was the recommended dish of the day, but I didn't fancy it much. Opted for spaghetti Bolognese instead. Not very adventurous, but then there'll be plenty of time for that later. Felt like Cinderella at the ball. One moment I was an English Second Division player who'd missed out on promotion, the next I was being treated like royalty. Shook hands with Farina but didn't get much out of him. Just as well because when he did try to speak English I couldn't understand a flaming word! He had that smouldering power about him. You could sense he was an important man. I was struck by the way they dress around here. Everyone's superbly smart – beautifully cut suits, silk shirts and ties.

Next morning there were a few formalities to see to. The medical check-up went well. When we came out into the street, the heat hit me like a grill! Nearly a hundred in the shade and very humid. Playing in this climate might be a problem, though they tell me the winters are pretty cold. Milan's getting ready for its summer holiday in August when everyone disappears to the mountains or the coast. The city lies in a valley with no winds to keep it cool, so August is reckoned to be unbearable. Only the wild dogs are left to roam the streets, apparently.

Next stop was the Villa Communale for the official reception with the club sponsors. The crowds were unbelievable. Most of them could hardly have heard of me and probably had no idea how to pronounce my name, yet they treated me like a film star. Ray too. My first experience of the Italian press. Boy, what a pack of hounds they are! Reporters and photographers were everywhere, you almost expected to see one pop up out of a manhole to get a different shot. They asked me every question under the sun. Santin did the translating and Ray and I did our best to answer them. They wanted to know every detail of my family life; my personal likes and dislikes; how many injuries I'd had and what sort – surprised they didn't ask for my inside leg measurement! Liedholm was there, parrying questions with the expertise of a man who does it every day. After thirty-odd years in Italy I suppose it was second nature to him. His Italian was quick and fluent. To my ears, it's just a babble of sound. Wonder if I'll ever talk like Liedholm?

He gave me a little speech about birth signs. He said Scorpio (my sign) was a great one for footballers. According to him, Pele and Rivera were both Scorpios, along with many famous war leaders. Struck me as a strange thing for a manager to believe in. I'd have thought he was too hard-bitten to be a star-gazer.

Didn't have much chance to talk to him because of the crowds. We shook hands for the photographers, but that was about all. I've already had an invitation to the Italian Riviera though. The club vice-president was very friendly and asked Ray and me to bring our families to his place at Alassio for a few days. Nice of him.

When we boarded the coach again to go back to the hotel, the streets were solid with supporters. Never seen anything like it. We'd only been there an hour or so and the centre of Milan was paralysed! The traffic cops were rushing about begging club officials to get the reception out of the way as quickly as possible so they could reopen the roads. Is this what it's going to be like?

Next morning, the papers were full of it. My picture was splashed all over the front pages. In the *Corriere della Sera,* one of the leading newspapers in Italy, I even knocked the Pope off the front page. He'd been making some official visit to Milan, but could only command a few paragraphs and a picture on the inside pages. And this in a Catholic country!

I've a feeling I'm going to like it here. There's nothing like fanatical support to bring the best out of an entertainer. If they love us so much now, what are they going to do when we start winning? I should think that if you get on the right side of the fans, the sky must be the limit.

Got back home with my head swimming, but the feeling was good. Can't wait to get playing, and prove to them that I'm not another Jordan or Blissett. Those names kept cropping up. I think the Milan fans are a bit touchy on the subject of British strikers after two successive failures. Looking forward to coming back here with Bev to find somewhere decent to live. Milan itself looks like a jungle. They tell me the lakes are beautiful.

Friday, 6 July

Bev and I have spent four days looking around the area. It's a big relief to get out of the city, but at the moment I can't see where we can live and bring up two young daughters. After a quick drive around the country areas, we get the impression that Italians don't bother that much about where they live. When I showed the photographs of our house on Hayling Island, they thought it was out of this world. It was a nice place with four bedrooms, but nothing exceptional in England. Goodness knows where we find anything like that here. Neither of us cared for the suburbs of Milan. It's all apartments – not a garden in sight. Where do the kids play?

An Englishman's home is his castle, but an Italian's is just a roof over his head. We think nothing of having four or five bedrooms, but here, a whole family will live in a three-room apartment. I can see this could be a real problem. Still, Liam Brady and Rummenigge have managed to get smashing places on Lake Como. Must go and have a look when we get a chance.

Had a few days back in England selling the house. That went well – sold it for £75,000 in three weeks. With Portsmouth paying off our £50,000 mortgage, it's all savings. Dennis has advised me to invest the money in more property in England.

Saturday, 21 July

The moment of truth. Reported for training today at a place called Brunico, up in the Alps near the Austrian border. What a terrible experience. We spend three hours in the morning running up and down mountainsides and through woods and gorges. Then it's back to camp for lunch between 1.30 and 2.30 p.m., followed by two hours' rest before we're out training again from 4.30 p.m. until 7.30 at night. Never been so knackered! First day today and I got a terrible cramp. The trainer told me to go easy for a couple of days. With pleasure!

Couldn't help wondering what the hell I'd let myself in for. Then I thought about the security I'd just achieved for myself and my family and ran even harder!

Security's the biggest worry in a footballer's life. Even though I'm only twenty-three, I think about it all the time. When you know that injury could finish your career tomorrow, you're bound to think these things. If you're lucky you get to thirty, but if you're Steve Coppell or Kevin Beattie, you can be finished early and in trouble. Who wants to start again in a new career that he's had no preparation for? If I'm intelligent with my money, I shouldn't have to work again after hanging up my boots.

This is what they call 'ritiro' (seclusion). We're to spend

three weeks at the training camp, living together and getting to know each other. It's strange being away from home and family for so long, but I'm keeping in telephone contact with Bev and the girls. They're staying at the Principe on the next floor from Ray's wife Jackie and their son, Ross. It's good to have Ray here. We can share our problems. Luther must have had a nightmare time on his own.

Friday, 27 July

First friendly match. Have been banging in the goals in training and am starting to feel really good. Incredibly, I've put on four pounds despite the intense hard work. Whether it's the pasta that's done it or running around with a stone of sandbags tied to my body I'm not sure. I thought I was a fit bloke before, but I'm really flying now.

Played the local team, Brunico, in front of 5,000 spectators. Couldn't have gone better for me. We won 11–0 and I scored twice in the first half. I also set up two others before taking a rest at half-time. The great thing is that the lads are supplying me with plenty of crosses. I've told them I survive on crosses. If they can fling over a dozen per game, I reckon I can get on the end of at least two of them. Will they keep it up though? Liedholm says in the *Gazzetta dello Sport* that he isn't at all surprised by my ability. He knew I was strong in the air and is delighted that I've shown how skilful I can be on the ground. Farina the president goes even further. He says he wouldn't exchange me for Rummenigge now!

Taking it all with a pinch of salt. The papers make a story out of anything and they do have a habit of exaggerating.

Sunday, 5 August

Our second pre-season friendly goes even better than the first. A team called Il Bolzano are the opposition – stronger than Brunico, but we won 5–1 and once more I scored two goals in the first thirty-six minutes. It's looking good, but as I keep telling the reporters, it's only a friendly. Let's wait till the season starts before we get excited. (Might as well tell a baby not to cry!) I took a bit of a knock in the game which ruled me out of the next couple of friendlies.

Wednesday, 22 August

Back in action with the winning goal against Parma in the Coppa Italia. Feel as though I'm settling in well. I seem to have become a legend in my own lunchtime and am getting mobbed most places I go. The club tells me the phone hasn't stopped ringing with fans offering villas with gardens. They know what I'm looking for.

The sooner we find a home of our own, the better. The Principe di Savoia is very good, but we can't live like this for much longer because the kids and Bev are cooped up too much. I'd have thought Milan would have been in a hurry to sort something out themselves. It must be costing them an arm and a leg to keep my own and Ray's family here. A single room is £850 a week with no meals included. Ray and I have both been given large doubles. Had a steak last night for dinner and that cost £45 without the trimmings! A bottle of Coke is £4.50! Ah well, if that's what Milan want, we just keep putting everything on the room bill.

Signor Fougier, the public relations officer, has been showing us a few possible places to live around Milan. He's a nice bloke and speaks English well, but Bev and I are bitterly disappointed with the apartments they've been suggesting. All of them are useless for a family of four. There's no way we're going to drop our standards. The Italians may prefer to spend their money on cars and clothes, but, as I keep telling them, I'm a family man and a good home is top priority. Ray feels the same. I bet Brady and Rummenigge didn't have these problems.

We've been here a month now, and I'm still driving about in a clapped-out Fiat hire car. The damn thing has no brakes, no tread, no nothing, and I'm pounding it into the ground. If they can't give me the car they promised me, I'm blowed if I'm going to take care of this heap! Farina's been trying to fob me off with a Golf, but I've told him I want a Mercedes estate or a BMW as promised.

Even more astonishing is that we haven't been paid a single penny yet. Goodness knows why. Can't get any sense out of anyone. I'm in the ridiculous position of having to take a five million lire sub (about £2,500) until I get my first pay cheque. I've opened an account at the Banco Agricolo Nazionale and am getting used to writing out cheques with bunches of noughts on the end. Feels like monopoly money! They're very strange when it comes to business, these Italians. They can't seem to get anything done in a hurry. It's all promises and 'We'll sort it out tomorrow'.

Sunday, 26 August

My debut at the San Siro stadium. Running out into that wall of sound made the hairs stand up on the back of my neck! Incredible! What it's like when it's full I can't imagine. Got kicked up in the air by the defenders in a friendly against Brescia. In the last minute, some guy called Chiodini goes down like a sack of potatoes and the ref sends me off for head-butting. We didn't even touch, though I must admit we came close. Chiodini had been baiting me all match and came gunning for me. As he did, I just dropped my head expecting him to make contact. Instead, he went rolling all over the floor as if I'd half-killed him. A real Royal Shakespeare Company job, that was, but the ref was fooled and off I went. Funnily enough, the fans seemed to like a bit of aggro. It might not be a bad thing to have asserted myself already. That'll probably terrify defenders. Somehow I don't think they'll be as keen to mix it with me next time. Word will probably get around that I'm some kind of maniac. I gather you don't do that in Italy.

Tuesday, 28 August

On the carpet in front of Rivera today. Through Fougier, he warned me not to react to provocation which goes on all the time in the Italian league. Point taken, but I think it's not a bad thing to show that I mean business. Ray sounded a warning note too. He said I should control my temper otherwise I could get into serious trouble.

The newspapers gave me plenty of support. Through them I officially apologised to the Milan fans for getting sent off in my home debut. Liedholm backed me up saying: 'He was subjected to a stream of fouls which the referee chose to ignore. This will serve to help him acclimatise to the Italian way of football.'

Wednesday, 29 August

Another pre-season friendly at Carrara, but didn't score. A pretty tame performance all round to be honest. After that, my two-match suspension arrives . . . and so, at last, do the keys to a new apartment at Legnano. It's not much of a town, but it's just off the autostrada between Milan and Varese, and only twenty kilometres from San Siro. The club has asked us to have a look and see what we think. Beginning to despair of finding the right place. The other day, some chap came up to the training ground saying he had a couple of places on Lake Como for Ray and me. They were much cheaper than Brady's pad and he reckoned he'd given the club all the details. When we checked back, Fougier told us the villas were out of the question – too expensive.

This is how it's been. We see somewhere, the club lets us look around, then tells us we can't have them.

Wednesday, 5 September

Less than two weeks to the start of the league season and after suspension I'm back in action scoring Milan's goal in a 2–1 defeat by Udinese. Not a good game again. Worried about the lack of service I'm getting. The goal came from just about the only chance we created. In between matches, the training at Milanello is hard but enjoyable. Am getting to know the Italian lads. Most are incredibly helpful. No animosity or bitchiness because we're foreigners and probably better paid than most of them are. Get on best with Galli, the defender I bashed all around the park in the Under–21 international; and Andre Icardi, my room-mate at Milanello. Both speak pretty good English. Some time soon I must get around to learning Italian. Am picking up a few basic words, but the temptation is not to bother because you can get by in English.

Liedholm only speaks a little English, but I get on very well with him. I think he sees in me the type of centre-forward he used to be – a good header of the ball with a strong left foot. He takes charge of all the football coaching and is a real revelation. He's a ridiculously young sixty-three, but when he takes the goalkeepers for shooting practice you've never seen anyone strike a ball harder in your life! We seem to have a good understanding. Don't know many of the tactical words in Italian, but he gets his message across.

Thanks to his coaching, I'm already a better player technically. Straightaway, he started to work on my feet. He's got me moving them faster when receiving the ball, turning and carrying. He's taught me about 'having respect' for the ball, as he calls it, and concentrating for ninety minutes. No one in England ever approached it that way. Because I'm improving my control and speed of thought, my confidence is growing. Interesting how the boss took one look at me in practice and immediately cut down my running. All we hear about in England is mobility – moving all over the pitch, finding space and dragging defenders out of position. Liedholm's done away with all of that. All he wants me to do is be in the box and score goals.

He says my territory is down the middle of the opposition half within the width of the 'D' of the centre circle to the penalty area – no going out onto the wings, no chasing full-backs. It's a tiny area to operate in for ninety minutes, especially when you're getting kicked all over the place. There's no escape, but there's nothing like it for improving control.

Dad's been over a couple of times and he's the first to admit that I'm a better player than he was. Coming from him, I take that as a real compliment. Whether you liked him or not, he was one of the best English centre-forwards of his time.

9–12 September

A week before our first league match, flew back to England to report for the East Germany game at Wembley. After my three games on the South American tour I expected to be given the number nine shirt again. To my surprise and disappointment, Bobby Robson brings back Mariner. It didn't seem to make sense considering what he told me three months ago. The manager didn't say much by way of explanation so I just assumed he was being loyal to one of his old players. Nevertheless, I was pleased to get on the pitch, even though it was only for ten minutes at the end, substituting for Tony Woodcock. Almost as soon as I came on, Bryan Robson scored the winning goal. Hope it's just a matter of time before I get my chance again.

Thursday, 13 September

A big shock when we got back from England – we'd been turfed out of the Duca di Milano, the hotel they moved us to about five weeks ago. The rooms had already been pre-booked for a trade fair so, without warning, Ray and I and the families are being shunted up to Malpensa, miles out of Milan near the training ground. They've got a bloody nerve!

When we get there, it's a case of the sublime to the ridiculous. The Cardarmo hotel is neat and tidy but, to our fury, the club expects Bev and me and two screaming kids to live in one room! Ray gets the same treatment. The manager's a nice bloke trying to do the best he can for us, but what the hell Milan are playing at I don't know. Ray and I are absolutely livid. This is going to be sheer hell. Our only hope is that it doesn't last more than a couple of days.

At least the rest of the players made us feel welcome back. They said they missed me despite qualifying for the final stages of the Coppa by drawing 0–0 at Trieste. In training, worked especially hard in the build-up to the first league game on Sunday. Liedholm congratulated me on getting onto the pitch in the East Germany match. Yet another press conference. I told them I was feeling good, but not yet at my sharpest; that I was frightened of no one (keep saying that to instil a bit of fear); and that I hadn't come to Italy to collect red cards, whatever the referees might think. They asked me about the failures of Jordan and Blissett again, but I said they were a million miles from my thoughts. If the rest of the team could supply the ammunition, I assured them I would do the job Milan bought me for.

It would be marvellous to repay the fans with a win over Udinese. Zico will obviously be their danger man. Should think he's already done wonders for their morale. Won't be easy but I'm not nervous. If I wasn't nervous making my England debut in the Maracana, I'm not going to start worrying now. Just going to go out there and enjoy it.

4
NO HOME ADVANTAGE

Sunday, 16 September: Milan 2 (Virdis, Hateley), Udinese 2

Fabulous league debut. It was just like being back home – end-to-end football, chances galore, several goals disallowed and four scored. Personally, it couldn't have been better. I made the first goal for Pietro Virdis with a long run and pass. Could have scored myself but slipped the ball to him in front of an open goal and that was that. The second I *did* score myself with a far post header. The keeper and the defender came for the ball with me, but I got there ahead of them both. Disappointed that Udinese equalised at 2–2 when we should have won 3–1. The fans were terrific. Officially 85,000 but it must have been close on 100,000 really.

Rave notices are coming in thick and fast. Vattaneo, the Udinese centre-back, says in the *Gazzetta* that I'm the most gifted aerial striker he's met and that my goal reminded him of Bettega. As I might have expected, the sportswriters examine every tiny aspect of my game. Nucio Abrosetti goes to town in the *Gazzetta*. This is how he analysed my performance: 'Thirty-four touches (47 per cent positive); seventeen passes (70 per cent accurate); four dribbles (two positive); five goal attempts (two on target); three interceptions; one tackle (successful); fouls against, nil; fouls committed, one.'

Surprised he didn't count how many times I scratched my backside!

Tuesday, 18 September

Life at the Cardarmo is impossible. The kids have suspected chickenpox and Bev is in quarantine with them. She's just about going out of her mind and there's not much I can do to help. Daren't get too close because of the risk of infection. This is just about the last straw. Ray and I feel like packing our bags and going home.

Thursday, 20 September

Milan supporters woke up to sensational front-page news. Hateley and Wilkins were on the point of flying home to England. The *Gazzetta* story was given added piquancy by recollections of the early sixties when Greaves abandoned Italy mid-season and Law and Baker soon followed the same route.

Sick and tired of thumping their heads against brick walls, Roach and his lawyer, Peter Baines, decided the only course of action was to send this ultimatum to the club. It wasn't solely a question of proper living accommodation – Hateley still hadn't received a pay cheque:

> 20.9.84 16:48
> 325018 Milan 1
> FOR THE ATTENTION OF SNR CARDILLO
> We are lawyers representing Mark Hateley who has a contract with AC Milan dated 28 June 1984.
>
> You are in breach of contract as follows:
>
> 1. You have not made any payments of salary to Mr Hateley, which were due monthly.
>
> 2. You have not provided Mr Hateley with a suitable furnished apartment.
>
> 3. You have not provided Mr Hateley with a suitable motor car.
>
> If salary payments are not made within 7 days and we

Towering over Collovati to head the winning goal against our deadly rivals, Inter Milan. The best goal I've scored

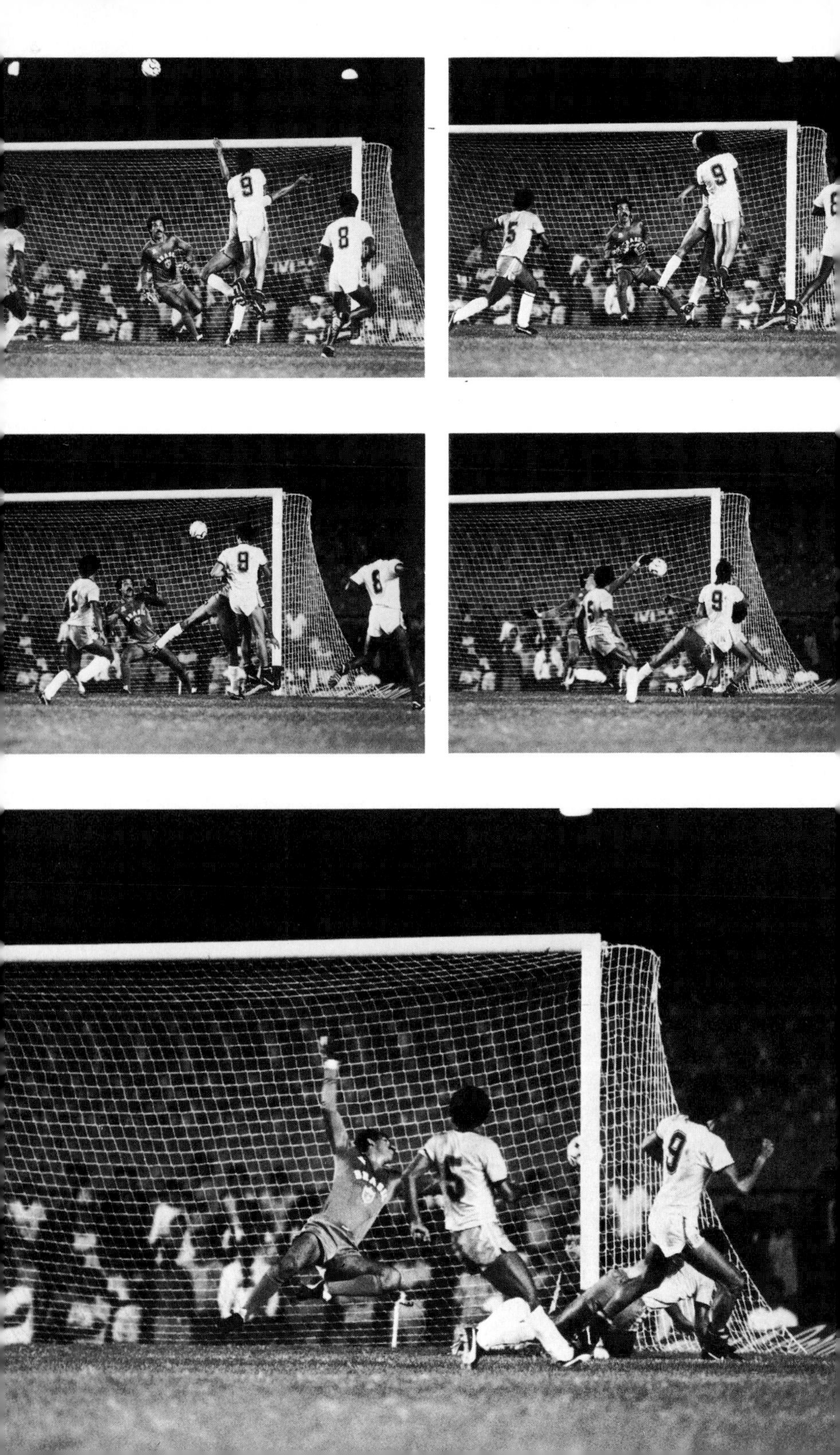

It happened in Rio. Little did I know these pictures were being studied frame by frame on Italian television

Above: It's not all sunshine! Ray and I clearing 8 inches of snow at Milanello

Below left: The Italians are scared to death of my aerial power

Below right: Nils Liedholm – made me a more complete player

are not satisfied that you are making proper efforts to supply an apartment and car, we intend to advise Mr Hateley that AC Milan are fundamentally in breach of contract and that he should return to the UK forthwith and take action in the courts for damages and breach of contract.
Pictons
11 Hatfield Road
St Albans
Herts
England

According to Baines, it was 'the only language they understand'. The ultimatum was received in Via Turrati with a mixture of complacency and arrogance, though subsequent newspaper revelations probably forced the club's hand. Milan were clearly embarrassed by the publicity and began tentative efforts, through its UK-based solicitor, Ron Teeman, to speed things up. Procrastination is a lovable characteristic of Latin countries, but not if you're on the non-receiving end for too long! Hateley was undoubtedly right to demand his rights, but to be fair to them, the club felt he was being a little unrealistic in his expectations. The newspapers had been full of stories about the luxurious accommodation provided for Rummenigge and Maradona, and an ambitious young man walking on streets he thought were paved with gold was ever-likely to have his head turned. The money Milan were being asked to find for his rent was twice the amount they'd allowed for Joe Jordan two seasons earlier. By the same token, Milan's disinclination to resolve the housing problem had cost them a small fortune in hotel bills. Beverley Hateley's laundry bill at the Duca di Milano, for instance, was £250 a week – money literally down the drain!

Part of the problem was Milan's misunderstanding of the role of agents. They weren't used to handling personal matters with a professional middle-man. Until the current crop of English footballers appeared on the horizon, agents belonged only to singers and actors. Italian players might bring along a brother or another relative to help oversee their discussions, but it was only an informal arrangement. Farina seemed to feel it beneath his dignity to engage in any dialogue with Roach, either in person or by telex.

There was a similar wave of mistrust blowing through English soccer at the time. The Football League was mildly embarrassed by the proliferation of agents since Dennis set up in business, and at least two club managers, Don Howe of Arsenal and Graham Taylor of Watford, felt compelled to speak out against it. The butt of their criticism was Frank Boyd, a Scotsman at that time acting on behalf of Mo Johnston and Charlie Nicholas among others. Taylor thought he was being manipulated by the agent, particularly in the transfer of Johnston back to Scotland, and Howe was furious about the exposure being given to Nicholas at a time when the so-called wonder boy was performing unspectacularly where it mattered.

Friday, 21 September

Dragged out of my sleep by the sound of Lucy choking in the middle of the night. Instinctively leaped out of bed, but couldn't for the life of me remember which hotel we were in. There'd been so many changes of address! In the pitch blackness, I hit my forehead against an archway in the bedroom wall. The blood came spurting out and I was spinning around like a stuck pig trying to find the light switch. Woke everyone else up in the process. Just another part of the nightmare. We thought two days of living like this in a small hotel would be more than enough, but there's no end in sight. It's a bad time for Bev because I'm away so much as well. We have this system called 'ritiro' where the whole team is locked away together sometimes for three days before a game. The idea is to keep our minds on the game, and to strengthen team spirit. Boring's not the word! There's nothing to do but eat, sleep and train.

Jimmy Greaves was slightly more caustic about the 'ritiro' system when he was with the club: 'Training camp – it was more like a prison camp . . . all it did was make the players sick of the sight of each other before a ball was kicked. It was like one long, boring game of follow-my-leader.'

It's the way football is out here, not so much a job, more a way of life. As far as the money men are concerned, footballers are assets like in any other industry. We are machines – and machines don't have feelings. In England, the best clubs cosset you and look after the family side of things, but not in Italy. For them, the family might not exist, which is strange because the Italians usually put the family above everything. Our players see hardly anything of their wives, girlfriends and children, but I make a point of taking Bev with me whenever I can. They're not used to that but it doesn't bother me. I don't see why a woman should be left out in the cold. It's so bad for the other wives that in the middle of the season, they pay for themselves to go away on holiday. I wouldn't like that. Having Bev and the girls around is a great comfort, and to me, the best times are when I get back home after a match and we can all be together. When I say 'home', I use the term loosely. We need a place very soon. Somewhere calmer and quieter where we can be ourselves. Dennis tells me he's sent telex after telex to the club threatening that I'll go back to England unless something's done soon. I'm fully behind him. It's a great shame to be in dispute because I love the club and the fans.

Sunday, 23 September: Fiorentina 0, Milan 0

My damaged head recovers well for the second game, at Fiorentina. So far, in the goal-scoring stakes, I'm ahead of Maradona, Zico, Rummenigge, Rossi . . . None of that famous brigade has opened his account yet! The second match did nothing to increase my tally. I don't remember getting a decent opening the whole game. We had one of our defenders, Tassotti, sent off early in the game, so it was a rearguard action after that. If ever a game was going to finish nil-nil, this was it.

Pleased with my performance, especially as Bobby Robson was in the stands. He had a quick word with Ray and me before the game and said how pleased he was that I was doing well in Italy. Afterwards, he popped into the team room to check that we were both okay. Feel confident of being named in the squad for the World Cup match against Finland next month.

Home situation goes from bad to worse. Thank goodness

Bev's able to phone her mum most days. Dennis is doing his level best to get things sorted out, but he can't get hold of Farina. The chairman has farms in South Africa and always seems to be away on business. Fougier is trying to help, but it's obvious where the power lies. Without Farina's say-so, nobody dares breathe!

Dennis Roach: 'I went to Milan three times in three weeks trying to sort out the accommodation problem. Each time, Farina was said to be away. Fougier's doing his best, but I can tell the club's being evasive. I only bumped into Farina once and he appeared not to speak English. Gianni Rivera was there too, but Farina's the only one who counts. Milan are a funny club to deal with. With Francis at Sampdoria, and Krol at Naples, there was none of this nonsense. I could have understood it better if Hateley hadn't been such an overnight sensation. Within weeks his value had shot up to £4.5m. He was arguably the most wanted player in Italy.

Not only that, he was guaranteeing big crowds at San Siro. The average price of a ticket there is £15, so each home game nets £2m. Then they complain that the apartments Mark fancies are too expensive! While Rummenigge and Brady live in luxury pads on Lake Como because they play for the other Milan club, Mark and Ray are stuck in a second-rate hotel. It made no sense. From a woman's point of view it was like being stranded in the desert. Bev was on her own in a hotel room for days on end with two crying youngsters. I take my hat off to Mark. Somehow through all that, he managed to carry on doing his stuff on the pitch.'

In the meantime I'm thrashing about in the Fiat still waiting for the Mercedes the club promised. It's not easy keeping your cool in a situation like this, but I'm trying not to let my anger and disappointment get in the way of the football.

Sunday, 30 September

At last I've received some money. Dennis's ultimatum must have got through to them, though when I asked around, I found that no one gets paid for three months until the end of September. If they'd warned me of that in the first place, things would have been simpler. Still don't understand the system. It seems that the rest of the players are so well paid they can go for three months with no money. I wasn't prepared for it. No one has provided an explanation for the delay. The club joke is that Farina floats the cash on the money market for three months and pays us out of the interest. Still no sign of the car. Or the apartment.

Milan 2 (Hateley 2), Cremonese 1

Another tremendous day for me and the team. Went a goal down in the first half but all changed in the second. I scored twice in seven minutes. First one was a header from a cross by Di Bartolomei, and the second a left-foot volley from Icardi's cross. I enjoyed that one, and so did the fans. It was like an explosion of sound and made me feel twenty feet tall!

Rivera says he wishes he was still young enough to play alongside me with Ray prompting from behind. I'm still ahead of the other top strikers in the league, which is all they seem to bother about here. If you score goals as regularly as Gunnar Nordhal or John Charles, they give you the earth. I've a long way to go to catch up with those two. The sport papers went mad again. Liedholm's quoted as saying that I'm improving all the time; Cattaneo, the Udinese defender, says: 'He's a real cyclone. Always on the lookout for the half-chance. When he jumps he seems to be suspended up there. He's accurate too and very quick with his shooting.'

Boniek has only seen me on TV, but he got in on the act as well. He reckons I'm the strongest header of a ball in the world. He thought I could finish up there with Platini among the leading scorers.

This is where I get my new name. The Italians never were any good at pronouncing Hateley. They *started* chanting 'Attlee' as though I was a former prime minister. Now, with encouragement from the newspapers, they've hit on 'Attila'. They think it's great and, of course, the English papers have cottoned onto it. It's all good publicity. I checked around to find out more about this fellow Attila. Which team did *he* play for? Apparently, he was a pretty fierce character who murdered his own brother and took the Roman empire by storm in the year 450 (about the time my dad was playing!).

Attila and his Huns invaded a bunch of Italian cities including Milan and ran amok everywhere they went. No wonder the Italians are a bit sore about him. The saying they have here is: 'Where Attila has been, the grass never grows green.' With my long hair and aggressive play, I guess they think the legend has come true again nearly two thousand years later!

I'm deliberately leaving my hair long to fit the image. They seem to like it. I hear from England that Brian Clough's been saying I should get it cut, but I don't think I'll bother.

Monday, 1 October

Getting nowhere with the apartment. Ray's found a smashing place near Legnano. There are forty-two luxury units with an underground swimming pool and a tartan tennis court. We've had a look and they seem perfect. Bev says she could be happy there. There's strict security round the development which is very comforting. Snag is, the club thinks the units are too expensive (about a quarter of a million to buy.) Must say I can't understand their thinking. Both Ray and I are playing out of our skins and still no co-operation. Beginning to wonder whether we're doing something wrong without realising. We've both come to the conclusion that the club has stopped bothering about us now that we're here. All those promises seem to stand for nothing.

Dennis and Peter send another ultimatum. The idea now is that if I don't get a suitable apartment in a week, I'll go back to England and commute.

1.10.84
12:45
325018 Milan

Mr Hateley tells us that he has now received payments of salary for the months of July and August 1984. He has not, however, received the Mercedes estate car which was agreed at the meeting with Mr Roach and you have not yet provided him with the four-bedroomed apartment in accordance with the contract. You promised that this would be available within seven days of the meeting, but we are informed that you now say it won't be ready for a further three weeks.

Furthermore, during the negotiations before the contract was signed it was agreed that Mr Hateley's legal expenses should be paid. Mr Roach tells us that you are now refusing to pay these.

Mr Hateley is very upset that he has still not been given an apartment. Would you please arrange for this as urgently as possible. Unless it is done, Mr Hateley may have to consider returning to England to his house here and flying out to Italy for each match until his contract is honoured. Regards,
P.W. Baines.

Eventually Milan agreed that we could have one of the three-bedroomed apartments at Legnano. They told us the three-bedroomed variety were the only ones left. Bev and I visited the site and were told a different story. There were four-bedroomed ones available. To my horror, Milan said they could only afford the smaller ones.

Wednesday, 3 October

Decided to take the law into my own hands. Ray and I both reserved our air tickets for London and marched into the Milan offices with wives and kids to give Farina one last chance. No bluff now. We were furious with the club forever belittling our problems. The business with the Legnano apartments has brought matters to a head. We left the wives and children in reception and called in to see Fougier first. After a brief chat, we insisted on seeing Farina. He may frighten others at the club but he doesn't frighten me. In the chairman's office, we were confronted by Cardillo and Rivera as well as Farina. Not being one to mince words, I dived straight in and accused Farina of neglecting us while we were playing our hearts out for Milan. I knew he spoke English because business interests meant that he spent half the year in South Africa. I told him it was about time he stopped pretending he couldn't understand the language. What did he speak when he was in South Africa – Swahili?

Ray and I tried to explain in our different ways the problems of a family living in a hotel. Ray's diplomatic approach was getting nowhere, so I interrupted and asked Farina how *he*'d like it with a young family – having to dress them up to go down to dinner each night. I told him that was no good for a child of Lucy's age. How she'd sit at the table throwing fistfuls of caviar and prawns at the other diners. Farina and his colleagues couldn't grasp what we were talking about – or more likely wouldn't. They asked why we were complaining about hotel life when everything was laid on for us. Hopeless!

The three of them ended up actually *laughing* at us. Nothing we said made any impact, and Farina tried to bring down the temperature of the meeting by referring to the greatness of Milan and handing me a book on the club's history. I jumped out of my seat and hurled the book straight back at him. That was enough for me. I told Farina I was buggering off back to England and slammed out of his office, nearly ripping the door off its hinges. I was so furious I had steam coming out of my ears! One thing I won't put up with is people laughing at me when I'm trying to discuss something serious. Ray tried to be more tactful, but deep down he agreed with me. We went back to tell the girls the bad news. Jackie and Bev both burst into tears. They'd set their hearts on the apartments. With the kids crying as well it was a terrible scene.

We were within seconds of walking out and catching a taxi to the airport when Farina opened his door and called us back in. He told us we could have the apartments after all. Just like that!

It was a moment Beverley recalls vividly: 'It didn't matter about the fabulous money we were earning. All we wanted to do was forget about Milan and get back to England with the family. It's the one time I've wanted to come home for good.'

From that moment, Farina and I knew exactly where we stood. We have a very strange relationship. People think we hate each other but that's not true. I respect him and think he respects me for speaking my mind. In a funny way I like him too, though the Milan fans haven't exactly taken him to their hearts. In fact, I get the feeling they'd be delighted to see the back of him. Since the blow-up about the apartment he refers to me as his 'son', and I suppose he's become a bit of a father figure to me.

Apart from that time, I've had no cause to fall out with him. That's the good thing about having Dennis as an agent. He does the falling out while I get on with the business of playing soccer.

5
CUT DOWN IN MY PRIME

Sunday, 7 October: Juventus 1, Milan 1

Had another good game in Turin. Great result for us considering the big guns at Juve. Heard so much about Platini and yet he hardly had a kick against us. He's obviously an outstanding player – you can tell from the way he moves and controls the ball – but this must have been one of his quieter days. Rossi didn't do a lot either, though his record as a goal-scorer speaks for itself. Not so long back, I would have regarded players like that as superiors, but these days I think they respect me as much as I do them. The press are virtually telling Bobby Robson to pick me for the Finland match.

Monday, 8 October

Day off. Decided to drive down to Venice. Took longer than we expected – three and a half hours on the autostrada. Gave the old Fiat a good thrashing – can't wait to get rid of it and have a real car. Little did we realise what was in store when we got to Venice. I was only out of the car for a couple of minutes before someone recognised me and I was submerged under a crowd. Incredible. I could have walked into Portsmouth Co-op a few weeks ago and no one would have batted an eyelid. I tried to slip away and hide down the back-streets, but it was hard work. Very flattering. We still managed to have a good day despite all the fuss. It's funny how your life changes once you get well known. We can't go out any more near Milan and it's not easy for Bev and the kids to accept that. Emma's started self-defence classes. Any time anyone comes close she punches them on the knees to keep them at bay. You watch little things like that and wonder where your private life's gone, but that's what it's like in Italian football and you just have to adapt.

It's a blessing that we've discovered a superb restaurant on the outskirts of Varese called Al Passatore. Varese's a town we've quickly grown to admire. The shops are smart, if expensive, with some magnificent clothes, especially for women. It's also far enough from Milan to keep the rowdiest supporters away. Outside Florence, they reckon Varese's the wealthiest town in Italy. I can quite believe it. A lot of Milanese businessmen have their villas around the edge of town. Some of them are staggeringly lovely with bigger gardens than I imagined could exist so close to the centre. We'd driven past Al Passatore while looking for Lake Varese. Bev said it looked too expensive so we didn't bother to go in. Later, Ray was going on about this marvellous restaurant he'd found where the owner spoke perfect English and the food was out of this world. Sure enough it was Al Passatore!

It's run by a chap called Giorgio Nizzardo whose wife, Evonne, comes from London. Apparently, it's the place to eat around here. Giorgio and Evonne used to have a place in Florence, and before that she ran a coffee bar in Paris, so she's known Europe pretty well. Giorgio's an avid Milan supporter, but he's not stupid with it. The most important thing for us is that he understands and respects our need for privacy after the madhouse of San Siro. He makes sure we can eat without being pestered. Ray and I go there regularly. In fact we're spoiled – I can't imagine wanting to eat anywhere else now we've found this. His home-made lobster pasta is magnificent – tagliallini all'aragosta! The girls can play in the grounds in perfect safety and Giorgio doesn't mind a bit.

That's one thing I've noticed about Italians – they put the kids first. It's quite normal to see little ones up until all hours at night having dinner with their parents. Giorgio positively encourages it. In fact, his ten-year-old son can drive the

Volvo! I agree with that. If you've got kids, why not let them share your life? Bev and I take ours everywhere within reason. If I had my way, I probably wouldn't send them to school at all. I never had any time for it, and I think I could teach them more about life. All you get at school is people shoving useless things into your head. Emma and Lucy will be allowed to do exactly what they want – blow exams and qualifications! If Emma wants to be a dancer or an actress, I'll encourage her all the way. Hopefully, we'll be financially independent by then and we can afford to take the chance. Her Italian's coming on well. She'll soon be better than we are. Keep meaning to get some lessons, but don't fancy sitting in a classroom and private fees are ridiculous. I can get by at the training ground with a mixture of Italian and English.

Wednesday, 10 October

Bobby Robson phoned to check on my fitness. He's naming his squad soon and says I'll be in it. I told him I was 100 per cent and raring to go.

Sunday, 14 October: Milan 2 (Di Bartolomei, Hateley), Roma 1

Brilliant result against the European Cup finalists. Liedholm badly wanted to win this one against the club he's just left and we did him proud. To rub it in, Di Bartolomei, who used to be the Roma captain, scored the first goal with a little help from me. Five minutes later I made it 2–0. One of the best goals I've scored this season. I saw Nela, the defender, in trouble and nicked the ball away from him. The way to goal was wide open so I kept going and smacked my shot inside the angle. That makes me joint top scorer in the Italian league with Serena from Torino.

Delighted with the way things are going. Can't seem to put a foot wrong. It would be fantastic to play for England now. People have told me the side looks a different proposition when I come onto the field. I think I made a good impression against Russia and East Germany, though I'm disappointed to be a substitute still. In the Russia game, the boss told me to go on and mess the goalkeeper around a bit. Not unfairly, just to let him know I was around. He pulled Mariner off because no one was challenging the goalkeeper, and we were losing without a whimper. Desayev was picking off the crosses like cherries from a tree. I soon put a stop to that. In the first minute, I hit him hard. He didn't get up for a long while. When he did, he stayed on his line and never dared to come out for another cross. When the goalkeeper's got other things on his mind besides the ball, he's in trouble.

I've decided that the only way to protect myself in the Italian league is to put myself around. Once defenders see that, they're not so keen to hand out the rough stuff. Referees give me hardly any protection, and that seems to go for most strikers. For some reason they favour the defenders. There's only one answer to that – be more aggressive. One of the reasons I'm doing so well here is that defences are terrified of me. I've got this reputation as a charging bull and they don't know how to handle it. One of the benefits of coming to Italy, apart from the money, is the chance to learn the style of football they'll be using in the next World Cup. That's my ambition, and if I'm accustomed to the continental ways I should be much more valuable to Bobby Robson.

After the Roma game, the fans were ecstatic, chanting 'Attlee' and 'Attila' and anything else they could manage. There were hundreds of them behind the railings where we leave. There was no way I could get to the car. Club officials had to bring it around to the back door. Ray and I were going straight off to Linate to catch the flight to England and things were even more chaotic at the airport. We had to have a police escort from the car to the terminal building otherwise we'd never have caught the plane. It was one hell of a rush.

Bev and the girls came with me to England. Charlie was at Heathrow to take them back up to Nottingham while Ray and I went off to High Wycombe to join the England party. Mariner is still injured so the boss is spared having to make the choice between him and me.

Wednesday, 17 October: England 5 (Hateley 2, Woodcock, Sansom, Robson), Finland 0

First taste of World Cup football went like a dream. It's taken longer than I thought to get another full international and I didn't intend to let the chance slip. The team played brilliantly – Finland are no mugs. Before the game, Thames Television had arranged for dad and I to walk out together in front of the Wembley crowd. It was a great moment for both of us. I like to think I'm very close to my father though I don't see him that often. There are only twenty years between us so we're more like brothers than father and son. We're on the same wavelength. When I first got into the England side then came to Italy amid all the publicity, I thought dad was jealous; as though he was re-living his past against mine. Strange feeling. It makes it difficult for us to feel completely at ease in each other's company. One of his best friends, Ken Simcoe, who used to play for Nottingham Forest, tells me that underneath the brash exterior, dad's chuffed to death with my success. I believe he is but perhaps he finds it difficult to show it.

Back to the game . . . and after trying to find a way through those congested Italian defences, playing against the Finnish back four was heaven. Enough room to drive a bus through! My first goal was a follow-up header, but the second pleased me most. It was a run through the defence followed by a shot – the sort of effort I might not have had the confidence to try before I went to Italy. I'd have been shooting from much further out where I didn't have to take on defenders. Two goals on my Wembley debut should keep me in the team for the next match at least. At this level, you can't bank on anything. I was pleased with my performance, but I know you're only as good as your last game. I had none of those Wembley nerves people go on about. I'd heard about the so-called pressure of playing for England at Wembley but I can't understand that sort of talk. Once you've reached the ultimate goal, it's pure enjoyment. Go out and savour it, I say. That way there can be no pressure.

Thursday, 18 October

Back at Bev's mum and dad's for a couple of days before the Naples match and Maradona! Bought most of the British papers this morning and I'm headline news across all the back pages. First time that's ever happened back home though it seems to happen in Italy all the time. Phone never stopped ringing with reporters and TV and radio stations wanting to do their follow-up stories while I was still in England. Why not? It's a novelty and fame doesn't last forever. Tried to fit them all in, and by lunchtime the drive was packed with cars and camera equipment. Quite funny how I've become an overnight celebrity in my own town; for twenty years they didn't bother with me.

ITV and BBC both wanted to film me eating fish and chips! All right by me because it's my favourite food anyway. Popped down to the local chip shop for my real lunch, then had to eat another couple of bagsful for the cameramen! To be honest, it's one of the things I miss over there, though there aren't many more. Also managed to nip into Nottingham for a spot of shopping. Bev prefers the Victoria Centre to anything in Italy. The clothes shops aren't as stylish, but at least she can browse without the pressure to buy. Once you set foot in an Italian fashion shop you know there's practically no chance of coming out empty-handed.

The prices in Italy are breathtaking. A shirt which might cost £30 in England will set you back twice as much. The average pair of shoes costs £75, and it's nothing to pay £500 for a suit.

Friday, 19 October

Left Heathrow for Naples to join up with the rest of the Milan team. Ray travelled with me, which is always a comfort. Whoever thought of bringing two Englishmen in together certainly did us a favour. There's always someone to share your problems with.

The Italian papers are full of stories about me again. They've quoted Bobby Robson as saying that Milan got hold of me just as my potential was developing. He thinks I'd have improved as much with an English club but I don't agree with the boss on that. Before I met Liedholm, no one paid much attention to my footwork. What I've achieved for England he must take much of the credit for. Liedholm has made my game much simpler and more effective by getting me to operate straight down the middle.

Sunday, 21 October: Napoli 0, Milan 0

Dreadful pitch! Torrential rain made it unplayable. The game would never have gone ahead in England. Not surprised at the result. Maradona didn't have a chance to shine and neither did I. Naples looks a down and out sort of place. Can't imagine Sophia Loren coming from here! In Milan, a lot of the waiters have migrated from the south for work. Northern Italy must be the best part of the country. I reckon Maradona's salary must account for more than half the Naples wage bill because there seems to be so much unemployment. They say the fans down here love entertaining football, so I suppose Diego's magic is just what they want to help them forget their problems. We're unbeaten after six games, though we've only won two so far.

Thursday, 25 October

Moved into the new apartment at Legnano. It's taken nearly four months to get this business sorted out, but here we are at last, thank God. The rest of the flats seem to be empty – I think they're a bit overpriced for the people round here. Smashing spot, though Legnano itself is nothing to write home about. We're pleased about the security arrangements. There's a gatehouse with monitors connected to remote-control cameras and an electronically operated iron gate. Very reassuring.

Sunday, 28 October: Milan 2, (Di Bartolomei, Hateley) Inter 1

This was the big one! San Siro was heaving with supporters from both clubs. We share the stadium with Inter, so the rivalry for the local derby is pretty fierce, you might say! This is a fixture to rival Liverpool and Everton, Manchester United and Manchester City or Spurs and Arsenal. Must have been 100,000 inside. One end of the ground is red and black, the other's blue and black and the noise they make is just deafening!

Bev's mother, Joan, came over to watch the game, but we couldn't get ordinary seats for them with the rest of the spectators – in other words, a cushion on a concrete step. That's typical of Milan's attitude to wives and family. I made the mistake of waving in their direction before the kick-off. Unfortunately, they were in with the Inter lot and as soon as they realised they were with me, the rabble started tossing cushions and drinks cans at them. Surprising, because normally the crowds are very well behaved.

Altobelli, the Italian international, put Inter ahead and after Di Bartolomei equalised, I headed the winner. Five goals in seven games now, but this was one of my best. Collovati, the centre-back for Inter and Italy, is one of the toughest opponents I've played against, so to get up above him was very satisfying. The crowd went mad. It makes your stomach turn over when you see that great wall of red and black stretching right up to the sky. Behind the goal, the fans have an enormous banner which they unfurl by passing it backwards over the heads of several hundred people. It's an astonishing sight.

Farina was beside himself. It's eight years since we last won a 'derby'. He says he thought he'd be a grandfather before we managed it again.

It's amazing what a goal can do! Took delivery of the Mercedes today – wonder if it's a coincidence! A turbo diesel in silver. Goodbye to the Fiat!

Inevitably, the *Gazzetta dello Sport* was moved to draw the comparison between Gunnar Nordhal, John Charles and Mark Hateley. It was a flight of fancy considering that Hateley had played only seven league games in Italy, but it made fascinating reading for the 'tifosi'. the *Gazzetta* invited Edmondo Fabbri, a former club coach, to analyse the three. He announced that Milan had found 'another Nordhal' but suggested that, whereas the Swedish star of the fifties was a genuine 'panzer', Hateley had more agility, mobility and bravery in the air. It makes one wonder whether poor old Nordhal had any qualities at all! And this is the man who for five consecutive years lorded it as the club's leading scorer – each season he totalled more than thirty goals!

Charles too had an impressive scoring record, especially by today's standards – ninety goals in four seasons with Juventus. The *Gazzetta* decided that there was a more distinct similarity between Hateley and Charles than between Hateley and Nordhal because of their aerial dominance. Fabbri came up with the following marks:

	Hateley	Charles
Right foot	8	8.5
Left foot	8.5	7.5
Heading ability	10	9.5
Shooting power	8.5	8
Physical strength	9	9
Dribbling ability	7.5	7.5
Temperament	8.5	8.5
Personality	8	9
Mobility	8.5	8
TOTAL	76.5	75.5

Wednesday, 7 November

Birthday boy. Twenty-three today. It's been the best year of my life. We've had a week off since the Inter 'derby'. Not much point hanging around in Milan so we all went 'home' to Nottingham. Always enjoy that. It was Joan's (Bev's mum's) birthday on 4 November, so we celebrated the two events together. Bev gave me a gold ring with nine diamonds in it – fabulous.

In the evening, we all went to 'Something Special', an expensive restaurant in town. Food was great but the place lacked atmosphere. We were the only ones there. Still, what can you expect on a Wednesday night? Nice quiet time and a pleasure not to be mobbed. No one in Nottingham pays that much attention.

Sunday, 11 November: Torino 2, Milan 0

Black day for me. My right knee went dead after a block tackle by Franchini. It hadn't been right since the Finland game. I'd felt something funny in the second half when I landed badly with the knee locked too far back. Came home feeling sore after that game, but didn't worry too much. I thought it was just a niggle – the type of thing you play with all the while. This time it went good and proper. No disguising it. I was in agony. Limped off with awful premonitions of a serious problem. The score was 0–0 when I left at half-time, but just to rub in the misery, Torino scored two second-half goals to hand us our first defeat of the season and knock us down from second place in the table.

I was so depressed that being singled out for the after-match dope test was the last thing I needed. The names of three players are drawn out of the hat each week and it's amazing how many times mine and Ray's name come up. The problem was that I'd been to the toilet when I came off and there was nothing left in the tank! I was in terrible pain with my knee and didn't know whether I was coming or going. I couldn't muster a sample no matter how hard I tried. The rest of the team sat in the coach for ages waiting to go home while I hobbled about outside trying to get cold so I could go to the toilet. Crazy situation. Eventually I managed it, but we didn't get away from the ground until nearly midnight. The rest of the lads were well pleased!

I've got no history of knee trouble. I dread to think what could be wrong. Knees are a footballer's nightmare. Once you've damaged them, they're rarely the same again. What a prospect!

Monday, 12 November

Doctor Ginco Monti gave me the bad news. He thinks I've shattered the actual kneecap. That means six weeks' absence, minimum, and goodbye to the England-Turkey match in Istanbul next month. A sickening blow this. One moment, everything's rosy, then it all collapses. Thought of dad and how his injury finished his career. Had a full examination and the doctor says he'll operate. Sends me to Verona to see a specialist friend of Farina's who confirms the diagnosis. No comfort to me, but vindication for Dr Monti who's clinging onto his position at Milan where Farina's trying to get rid of him. Not impressed with the medical set-up here. Milan want me to have the operation in Verona, but what the hell – it's my bloody knee and I'm not being dictated to. The specialist may be a pal of Farina's, but he's no pal of mine. He twisted the knee during the examination and made it worse! Told the club I want the op in Milan where I can be close to the family.

Tuesday, 13 November

Milan have a board meeting to decide where I shall have the operation. It's not their decision. Eventually, Cardillo and Rivera persuade Farina to let me have my way. Don't suppose Farina wants another showdown with me. I threw a book at him last time, there's no telling what I might do next, even with a gammy knee! I'm booked into the university clinic at Pavia not far from Linate airport. After talking to the surgeon, I feel much more optimistic. He's going to use laser-beam surgery which means he can mend the knee without actually opening it up. He reckons six weeks is the normal recovery time, but I want to get back in action as soon as possible. Liedholm is giving me all the encouragement. He says how much the team relies on me, not just for goals, but inspiration. That's good to hear.

Wednesday, 14 November

Operation day – the same day that England play Turkey. No prizes for guessing where I'd rather be. Surgery takes an hour and a quarter – not that I remember much about it! They showed me the hospital video of the operation and it did nothing to speed up my recovery! In the end they didn't use laser beams, but they were pleased with the way it went and with my recovery. It was pandemonium in the hospital. While I was still coming around from the anaesthetic, they allowed the television cameras in to film me. I didn't know anything about it of course. I'll let Bev tell the story.

'Mark had the operation at nine o'clock in the morning, but when I telephoned, they said I couldn't visit him until four o'clock that afternoon. So I waited. To my horror, I was watching the television at lunchtime when up popped a picture of Mark unconscious in his hospital bed. I couldn't believe it!

I waited until visiting time as instructed and walked into his room expecting to be alone with my husband. A fine chance of that! When I opened the door, the room was crammed with people. Nobody was saying anything. Deathly silence – apart from the clicking of two dozen cameras! Mark was lying there half-conscious, just managing to flick one eye open from time to time, but not knowing where he was. I went over to speak to him with this audience all around me. Most were photographers but the rest were just fans off the street.

It was ridiculous. I called the nurse and asked what all those people were doing in a private hospital room. Do you know what she said? – she hadn't been able to stop them coming in! What rubbish! I shouted at her to get them out at once. This went on for a couple of hours before they filed out under great protest.

Went to visit Mark again the next day. Thank goodness there was no one in the room – not at first anyway! For the next twenty minutes, I never got the chance to say a word to him. Nurses were coming in with patients bandaged up and in their dressing gowns wanting Mark's autograph. He was close to tears. He'd had enough of it. With the help of the surgeon, Boni, we got rid of them and persuaded the hospital to put a security man on the door so that Mark could have some peace. I went home relieved once I saw the chap sitting there with his peaked cap on.

Less than two hours later, Mark phoned to say he was coming home. The fans were pouring in just like before.'

I got out of bed to see what the hell the security man was playing at! He just shrugged his shoulders. It was obvious what was happening – the fans were bribing him to come in and see me and he was making a nice little living in back-handers. Then I found out that a television crew had been allowed in to film earlier in the morning while I was still out cold. That's what Bev had seen on the lunchtime news. We were absolutely disgusted and I told Boni I was going home. He said I couldn't because I was his responsibility and he needed me in hospital in case of complications. There was no way I was going to stay there. I was getting no rest. I virtually discharged myself and went home for some peace and quiet.

You would never have believed that this was supposed to be one of the foremost clinics in the world. Trevor Francis and Paulo Rossi both had leg operations there. Yet the standard of hygiene was dreadful and you could walk past the theatres and see people being operated on. They didn't even bother to shut the doors! I would have been better off in England, but that's with the benefit of hindsight. I just hope they've done the job properly and not left me with a permanent disability. The only nice thing was that I received around 500 get-well cards and telegrams, including one from Agnelli, the Juventus chairman, and another from Sancher, the president of Barcelona. Wonder why he sent one?

I got a telephone call from Bev to say that England had beaten Turkey 8–0. Fantastic news, even though I wasn't part of the celebrations. I had the feeling that we would murder someone soon! Peter Withe played instead of me because Mariner was still injured. He's a great bloke, Peter, but he must have been disappointed not to score once. I first met him at the Finland game and we got along very well. He's my type of player – a real battler. Strikers usually reach their peak at around twenty-eight. Peter reached his a bit later and just kept going. It'll be a great achievement if he gets to Mexico for the World Cup. Come to think, the way I feel, it'll be a great achievement if *I* get there!

In the meantime, while Hateley was regaining consciousness seemingly in full view of the whole of Italy, the two consultant professors, Boni and Farina's ally, Marega, were trying to pour oil on troubled waters.

The idea of two learned medical experts bickering over who would perform an operation and where, is almost too bizarre for words. The pair finally admitted as much in a statement issued by Boni:

'We haven't exactly covered ourselves in glory with this operation. We deal with dozens of similar cases but it was a great pity that so much was written and said about the disagreements. We would like to close that chapter once and for all.'

6
ROCK BOTTOM

Saturday, 8 December

No sooner was one controversy over than a new one took its place, hitting the football fraternity of Milan like a thunderbolt. A mere three weeks after his operation, the news burst upon an unsuspecting public that their hero was on the ski slopes, no less! Not only that, but it was the club vice-president, Gianni Nardi, who'd arranged the trip. Nardi and Farina weren't the best of friends but Nardi, unfortunately for the chairman, held too big a financial stake in Milan to be nudged aside. The wealthy number two at Via Turrati had invited Mark and his family for a weekend at Sestriere in the Italian Alps, having first sought permission from Liedholm and Dr Monti. What Nardi had neglected to mention was the ski-ing! Hateley, as one would expect, was enthusiastic about the excursion, even if his wife could see the other side of the coin.

It was a welcome break from the monotony of getting over the injury. As far as I was concerned, the knee was healing well. I'd reported back for training only twelve days after the op. I felt a little pain, but no one objected to me running around the football field and kicking a ball. As soon as it came to ski-ing, all hell let loose! I'd never seen a ski resort, so when I was invited, through Nardi, to present the prizes at the world downhill slalom championships, I jumped at the chance. Italian footballers do a lot of ski-ing. Rossi even has a house in Sestriere, so what harm was there in my having a go? I was due to play on the Sunday, so I didn't see any harm in trying the slopes on the Thursday before. It was something I wanted to do so I did it.

The players are mollycoddled. You'd think they didn't have a mind of their own. Well, I'm not a child. Farina and Cardillo were furious; they hate Nardi anyway. The chairman slaughtered me in the newspaper, but neither of them dared confront me face to face. Cardillo knows I'd knock his block off if he tried.

Beverley Hateley:
'When Mark gets an idea into his head, there's no point trying to talk him out of it. It would never have been allowed by an English club. I thought he was wrong to go, but it was up to him. I can quite understand the club's dismay.'

I didn't have a clue about ski-ing but Nardi fixed us up with a brilliant instructor called Piero Marcellin. He took things gently so there was no danger. I wasn't going to risk my career for the sake of a bit of snow, was I?

Bev and I were showered with gifts. The representative from Ellesse was there giving us all the ski clothes we could carry, and Rossingnol were practically throwing skis at us.

Unfortunately, they weren't the only people interested in my visit. The perishing photographers were out in force. Can't blow my nose without one of them getting the picture! I'm not kidding, there were some blokes with three cameras strung around their necks, all decked out in ski gear ready for the chase. When we tried to throw them off the scent, they'd appear from behind a tree. Needless to say some of the reporters managed to pin me down. I told them what I've written here. That and a few other things!

There was one photographer who was a professional skier and he took it upon himself to stay with us wherever we turned. The instructor had had a bellyful of the bloke (as I had), so he decided to send him packing in the most devastating way. Piero was ski-ing backwards down the mountain watching my descent when he caught sight of the photographer not far behind him. One quick look over the shoulder, a subtle change of direction and Piero was heading straight for the poor chap. Without stopping, the instructor skied straight through him backwards and knocked him flying. We shouted to him to clear off and he staggered away battered and bruised with his film ruined. Served him right!

Apart from having a go at me, Farina accused Nardi of trying to make a name for himself by acting outrageously. He thought Nardi had pulled a fast one, which, in a sense, he had. Farina asked in the *Gazzetta* whether Milan should perhaps change its training schedule to fall into line with Nardi and introduce pre-ski practice. Sarcastic bugger!

As quickly as it had blown up, however, the matter was forgotten and dismissed by Farina as 'a mischievous prank'. On hearing that Hateley was back on target in training, the chairman was moved to say: 'He's a nice lad. How can you get angry with him?'

Sunday, 16 December: Milan 2, Atalanta 2

Promised the fans I'd be back before Christmas, and here I am, only thirty-two days since the operation. The doctors are amazed and so is everyone else. I told them it was the ski-ing which brought about the miracle! That went down like a wet sandbag!

Their six weeks forecast, I discovered, was an optimistic one. When I left the field against Torino, we were unbeaten. Milan lost that game and haven't scored a single goal since I've been out. The papers want me to say that the side can't hit the net without me playing, but it's not as simple as that. They're no more a one-man team than any other. In fact they've done quite well without scoring. The two away draws at Avellino and especially Verona were very good results and no one can say we deserved to lose at home to Sampdoria. Trevor Francis scored the only goal from a last-minute penalty. Dad came over to see me that weekend. It was pre-arranged and the only time he could get off so it was a great shame that he didn't see me play. Don't think he can make it again until next winter.

It's a real joy to be part of the team again, though we should have beaten Atalanta if we want to make a serious challenge for the title. Being injured is like being in prison.

You get ill-tempered and bored. It's not as if you can pop out and see a few friends like you can in England. Although I've missed three games, Platini is only two goals ahead of me.

What a frustrating match! We were two up inside half an hour and threw it away. I didn't score, but was fairly happy about things until I got a knock on the knee near the end of the game. Came off with five minutes to go feeling tired. Not match fit. I missed a couple of chances through lack of sharpness, but the fans were incredible. They nearly brought the sky down when my name was announced on the team sheet! Atalanta crept back into the game and Gentile went and grabbed an equaliser from nowhere.

The knee didn't hurt too much, but it was swollen after the game. Don't say I've got to go through all that again!

Tuesday, 18 December

My worst fears seem to be confirmed. I wake up each day with the knee swollen and aching badly. The doctor drained off about six inches of blood from it today. He says it was a burst capillary vessel. Don't like the sound of it, though Dr Monti says there's nothing to worry about. How can there be nothing to worry about when they're draining blood from the joint? Don't trust these Italian medics. They seem to make such wild guesses and hope for the best. Monti says to rest for a few days. Here we go again. This hanging about with nothing to do will drive me up the wall.

Wednesday, 19 December

Had enough of this. The knee's still causing a lot of trouble – swollen and aching, but can't get any sense out of the doctors. All they talk about is draining it. Can't they see that there must be something more seriously wrong than a burst vessel? Got in touch with Dr Pearson, a specialist in Birmingham, to make an appointment. Need the opinion of someone who knows his job. I've no chance of playing against

Ascoli on 23 December, so there's no point in hanging around here. I've got an appointment in Birmingham which might sort the whole thing out once and for all, so Bev and I left for England before the club Christmas party. It'll be a bitter-sweet Christmas. Bitter because I'm letting the fans down by missing Sunday's game, and sweet because in seven years as a pro, I've never had Christmas at home with the family. Looking forward to that.

The truth of the matter is that I rushed back into action much too soon, but the club was only too eager to let me. I did it for the fans. A case of letting my enthusiasm run away with me. I'd have done better to wait until the New Year. We don't have to report back until 5 January, so I should get a good rest in Nottingham.

In the meantime, Farina is beating his brow once again over Hateley's allegedly unannounced departure to England. He takes it as a personal slight and, as is his wont, goes into print regretting that Hateley saw fit to 'turn his back on the club's Christmas party'. The *Gazzetta*, a Farina mouthpiece, quotes him like this:

'I didn't give him permission to leave. Why did he decide to slip away so fast when all the arrangements had been made? Ray Wilkins and his wife were there with the rest of the team. Why should Mark Hateley be a law unto himself? I wonder who he thinks he is!'

The *Gazzetta* piece is a load of eyewash. I didn't stay for the party because I had an appointment with the specialist in Birmingham. Farina thought it was more important for me to wear a paper hat than get my knee sorted out. It shows how unthinking he is. I made the appointment a week before the party and was relieved to have got in to see the specialist so soon. It was for the good of the club, as well as myself, that I did it. They knew very well I was leaving. I told Liedholm the day before the party not to set a place for me at the table. Farina seems to want to pick an argument about everything and the papers are dead keen to encourage him. It's all so petty. I wonder if the chairman realises how silly he's making himself look wingeing about a Christmas party?

Thursday, 20 December

Back at Joan and Charlie's after a good flight. Press were at Malpensa airport to see me before I set off and I gave them a few quotes. Nice to get away from it all for a while.

Back in Nottingham, went with Bev and Emma to buy all the Christmas presents. The great thing about shopping in England is that hardly anyone recognises me. Dashing around from store to store with literally thousands of others. Thank goodness Christmas only comes once a year! Good atmosphere in town. Looking forward to having a Christmas like everyone else. For lunch we popped into MacDonald's for a juicy hamburger. That's one of the things I miss about Italy. Their food is terrific but very rich. Nice for a change just to eat something simple like hamburger and chips!

Walking around the shops hasn't done the knee a lot of good. Had to rest up when I got back to Charlie's. This doesn't look very promising. I've made arrangements to see Doctor Pearson at Coventry City. The club's been extremely helpful, making all their facilities available to me for as long as I need them.

Friday, 21 December

Charlie took me over to Coventry in the Jag. Doctor Pearson examined my knee and says he doesn't want to start any treatment until the swelling has disappeared. He's told me to rest as much as possible then we can begin working the thigh until it's strong enough to support the knee again. Such a relief to get some sensible advice – and in English!

Popped into Paul Todd's in Coventry to get my hair cut – first time I've bothered since going to Italy. By coincidence bumped into my old Coventry pals, Ian Butterworth and Perry Suckling. From what they tell me, things don't change much at Highfield Road. If Coventry don't get relegated this season I'll be very surprised. They've done the Houdini act for about ten years now – surely they can't keep getting away with it?

Bought the last of the Christmas presents including a ring

for Beverley's brother and a microwave oven for Joan and Charlie. Then it was out for a meal with a couple of friends from Nottingham, and a late night at Madisons night club where we met Tony Woodcock and his wife. First time I've spoken to him at length. We swopped stories about football in Germany and Italy. He wondered if I could get him out to Milan!

Sunday, 23 December

Relaxing day at Charlie's. Watched soccer highlights on television. They showed Portsmouth versus Oxford and I was delighted to see Portsmouth win 2–1. Alan Biley got both goals. Good old Alan! It would be great to seee them promoted this season. Finished the day with a good old-fashioned Nottingham curry. Can't get anything like this in Italy.

Monday, 24 December

Can't believe there's still Christmas shopping to do, but women always think of something at the last moment, don't they? Starting to feel a bit ropey – and I don't think it's the effects of the curry. I'm not the only one under the weather. We stayed in all afternoon and evening – no energy.

Tuesday, 25 December

Emma and Lucy were thrilled to bits with their presents, just like several million other kids all over the world. The Christmas spirit was definitely missing, however, because the whole family seems to be coming down with flu. It was all we could do to sit in the armchair watching TV. The highlight of the day was watching Harrison Ford in *Raiders of the Lost Ark*. As for turkey and Christmas pud – none of us could touch it. We were too busy being sick. I didn't swallow a drink or a bite of food all day. The worst Christmas for as long as I can remember!

Wednesday, 26 December

Feeling much better – that is until I went out for a lunchtime pint with Charlie and my friend Jim who's up from Portsmouth. Had to rush home and could hardly lift my head off the pillow. No better in the evening. We all went out for a meal but I couldn't eat a thing.

Thursday, 27 December

What a carry on this is. Popped into town with Bev to change my leather trousers. I had to keep rushing outside to be sick. If the Milan fans could see me now!

Friday, 28 December

My salary payment arrived. Left Nottingham at 5.30 a.m. for Heathrow to pick up the flight back to Milan. Christmas is over – in fact it didn't seem to get started. At least my knee has been rested and doesn't seem too bad. Arrived back in Milan to find eight inches of snow! No one can remember when they had it this bad. The roads were clear so I was able to get to Via Turrati in the city centre to collect the car. From there I reported directly to Milanello to see the doctor about my knee. Exercised my knee and thigh and everything okay. No swelling. Doc advises nevertheless that I continue to take it easy and don't go on the club trip to Sicily. Went around to Ray's in the evening and stayed the night – not much point staying alone at our apartment. Bev arrives the day after tomorrow.

Saturday, 29 December

Went into Varese to buy food at the big department store, Standa, ready for Bev and the girls coming back.

Monday, 31 December

Looking forward to welcoming New Year with the family. My sister, Tina, has come over from England with Bev. We've arranged a party in the residents' bar at the apartment. About twenty-five people coming. Liam Brady and his family have been invited too. This is my last entry of 1984. It's been a good year with so much happening it was difficult to keep pace. If 1985 is half as good, it'll do for me.

Tuesday, 1 January 1985

A struggle to get up today after a great party. We had two bites of the cherry – seeing in one New Year at midnight, Italian time, and another at 1 a.m. with the rest of Britain. Glad to get to bed after an extremely early morning. Recovered sufficiently in the day to take my sister to Lake Como for the first time. She was duly impressed even though most things were closed during the national holiday.

2–6 January

Back at the training ground for the moment of truth. Would my knee stand up to it? On the first day I ran for half an hour by myself in the snow and later went to the multi-gym for muscle-building exercises. The illness over Christmas has left me pretty weak, and four pounds underweight. At the gym, they put a drip in my arm for half an hour, dosing me up with multi-vitamins to bring back the strength.

The ground is very hard at Milanello, frozen to quite a depth, which makes it extremely tough going on the knee. In fact, it became too sore for me to train. The drip-treatment continues but this is a very difficult time for me after all the early success. There's so much uncertainty about the knee – one day it's good; the next it's back to square one with sharp pains just like the worst days. The injury's preying on my mind terribly. Things like this make you realise how easily it could all end.

Early tactical talk from Dad – he wanted me to follow him

Boots flying at Coventry. Ray Ranson is about to join me on the deck

Above: Reconciliation: we line up with the Italy players in a silent tribute to those killed in Brussels

Below left: TVS poster – I'd love to go back to Portsmouth one day

Below right: Tête-à-tête with Southampton's Mark Wright during FA Cup battle at Fratton Park

Above: Oscar-winning performance by Udinese's Marco Billia who tries to get me sent off

Below left: Ray's the first to congratulate me after my debut goal for Milan

Below right: Lean on me! Inter's goalkeeper, Zenga, comes off best this time

Above left: Money can't buy this. Lucy and Emma make it all worthwhile

Above right: The Hateleys and the Wilkins in Milan's cathedral square. Lucy wasn't impressed!

Below left: My prop and staff. Beverley comes with me everywhere

Below right: Rio at my feet... Milan is just a whisper away

Next match is in Rome against Lario, but my chances of playing virtually disappeared after a bad training session in Rome. The joint on the outside of the knee was so badly swollen I could hardly walk. The capital of Italy is a great city, even in this rotten weather. Ray and I took a taxi to see the sights. The normal places, St Peter's Square, the Vatican, the Parthenon. To fill time we called in at an English cinema, but the place was closed so it was sitting around the hotel signing autographs and having more treatment on the leg, not to mention the vitamin drip!

Sunday, 6 January

Should have played Lario today, but woke up with a blizzard blowing and four inches of snow already on the ground. The game was called off but we couldn't return home. What you have to do in Italy is hang around in case there's a chance of completing the fixture the following day. Highlight of a long and tedious Sunday was a snowball fight in the streets of Rome with the photographers snapping away for all they were worth. Later we called into the television centre, RA1, to watch Inter and Roma draw 0–0 at San Siro.

Monday, 7 January: Lazio 0, Milan 1 (Virdis)

Game went ahead on the Monday – without me. Not a bad match. Virdis's goal was smartly taken and only the crossbar prevented Ray scoring his debut goal for us. Spent the rest of the day travelling 350 miles back to Milan. For me it's a nightmare travelling to matches where I know I'm not going to be involved. I'd much sooner be back home out of the way.

Tuesday, 8 January

Emma started school. The biggest step in her life – and a big one also for Bev. Tense day. We knew there'd be lots of tears. Tried to play down the added problem of being among foreigners – it's hard enough for a youngster as it is. Ray's little lad, Ross, was starting at the same time. The two of them looked a treat in their new uniforms. As soon as they saw the other little kids running about, they didn't want to know. The nun in charge said we had to go away and leave them. Easy to say, not so easy to do, especially for Bev. This was the first time her baby was leaving her. We did what the nun said and collected them again at one o'clock. Then the tears came gushing back. Emma's Italian accent, we're told, is very good and Lucy's is bound to be. They tell us that Lucy may take longer to talk properly because she's hearing two languages all the time. Then, at about the age of four, it'll suddenly click into place and she'll be able to speak English and Italian fluently. Lucky girl!

Football seems a world away just now. The days just drag with nothing to do except hang around the house listening to my tapes and helping Bev with the kids. We can't even watch television and understand it, though most of the programmes are American cop series and English films. Bev's bursting to scribble a few words in the diary so here goes.

'I'd like to put on record that Mark is driving us all mad. He's restless and irritable and the sooner he plays again, the better for everyone!'

Friday, 11 January

Went training again today, but the ground is much too hard for the knee. The only topic of conversation is whether Sunday's match at home to Como will be on or off. Still mountains of snow around. I hope the match is off because my mind's not right. Tonight we're in 'ritiro' in the Jolly Hotel, Milan. Can't for the life of me see the point of staying away from home like this. It's a pain in the neck. Much sooner be home with the family.

Saturday, 12 January

Nothing to do in Milan so Ray and I did the foolhardy thing and went shopping in the centre. What a big mistake. So many autograph hunters and fans asking us to pose for photographs that it's impossible to move. The price of fame I guess. Our second mistake was turning into Monte Napoleoni Street! It's reckoned to be one of the most expensive streets in the world, full of designer shops like Armani, Missiori, Cerutti, Valentino – you name it, they're there! Fantastic clothes. No wonder Milan is the fashion centre of the world. It takes your breath away. After this, Nottingham's Victoria Centre won't seem the same.

Took the plunge and bought Bev a fur coat. Hope she likes it! Ray couldn't believe it – said I was a bit impulsive. I'd have to agree. Didn't tell Bev about the coat. Just told her on the phone that I'd bought a fluffy jumper.

Sunday, 13 January: Milan 0, Como 2

Bad result but a good day for me. For once my knee was perfectly all right and my mind felt at ease. First time I've felt that glow of confidence for a long time. The pitch was frozen solid and it started to snow just before the kick-off. I had the advantage of the rubber-pimpled boots I used for Astroturf in the States. A lot of the lads didn't have those.

After the game I presented Bev with the fur coat. She thought it was fabulous. That's a relief! (Didn't tell her the price until we got back home!)

The snow is getting ridiculous. Woke up next morning with two feet of the stuff outside. The kids love it of course. Surprised how severe the winter is. I think the Italians are too. To my delight, the knee feels brilliant after the game. No more pain, and, hopefully, an end to those irritable days! I feel ten times more relaxed and had a good lie-in to give my leg an extra rest. Impossible to describe what a weight has been lifted from my mind. Felt so good, I played outside in the snow with Emma and Lucy. Tried to build them a snowman but the snow was too powdery. Had an easy evening watching television as best we could. Thank goodness for the central heating!

Tuesday, 15 January

Snow continued through the night. It was three feet deep outside the terrace next morning but we were still determined to get Emma to school. She and Ross are very good now. A few tears to begin with, then smiles. I feel a lot happier about leaving them now. Ray and I have opted to take them each morning because the girls are too soft and can't tear themselves away. No good for the kids or the mums.

Took Bev's coat back to the shop to be altered. Only the sleeves, collar and back need changing – otherwise it's okay! While we were there, decided to have a hat made in the same material. I fancied a pair of shoes but being in the shop was like being in a zoo! About a hundred people gathered outside and were literally pushing their noses up against the glass. Goodness knows how international pop stars and film stars manage to get out of their homes if it's like this. I only have to put up with it in Italy.

Wednesday, 16 January

Ray and I took a hand with the snowplough at Milanello because the white stuff is still coming down in bucketsful. The pitch was only half-cleared when we came to play. It was bone-hard underneath but icy and wet on the top. A recipe for disaster if ever there was one, and sure enough disaster struck in the afternoon. I jumped for a ball and landed awkwardly with the knee stretched too far back. Shit! It would have to be the same knee, wouldn't it? Had to come straight off. All the nightmares about the injury came flooding back. Went to see the doctor and his verdict was: 'Rest.' The same old music!

In the evening, tried to forget the problems by having Ray and his family around for supper. It's a long walk from his place . . . all of 150 yards! We watched Juventus beat Liverpool 2–0 in the Super Cup and it helped to take my mind off things for a while. That man Boniek looks some player!

The relief didn't last long. Woke up the next morning with all the tell-tale signs again. The knee felt swollen even though I had a bandage on. I've had so many of those that I can tell exactly what's going on underneath. The stiffness was back and fluid was passing through the joint every time I tried to walk. My mind was in turmoil; the confidence-building week was shattered. Training was out of the question. All I could manage were straight leg lifts. God knows whether I'll be able to play on Sunday. The way I feel right now, it must be very doubtful.

Sunday, 20 January: Udinese 1, Milan 1 (Hateley)

After an eight-and-a-half hour coach trip to Udine, I was ready for one thing only – sleep. Yet I couldn't manage it. The knee was troubling me all night, but worse still, my mind doesn't feel right. I get to the stage where I don't know whether I'm imagining the knee or whether it's really very bad. If I was at home with the family, I could prepare myself much better for the game. Being away in strange hotels makes me depressed. Curiously enough, training this morning went well on a soft pitch and the leg didn't seem too bad until I caught a ball on the end of my foot. Then it hurt. When it came to the true test, everything was fine. Not only played but scored our only goal in a 1–1 draw. What inspired me were the hundreds of Milan supporters who'd made the long trip. They were around the hotel hungry for autographs and I didn't feel I could let them down. The game went very well for me. Dare I say it, the knee isn't giving any trouble at all.

Monday, 21 January

Celebration over – woke up with the knee feeling *terrible*! Pain internally and externally. I think the light bandage I'm wearing is thoroughly inadequate. A frustrating day from every point of view. Went to collect Bev's new car, a Golf GT Cabriolet. But the Italians ran true to form and sent us to the wrong garage! It doesn't bother them. After a while you learn to take it with a pinch of salt like they do. Tomorrow it'll be okay, so why work yourself up into a lather today?

Had the knee drained of fluid. The medics seem to think there's nothing unusual about it, but I can't help wondering why it should be necessary after all this time. What's going to happen the next time the fluid gathers, and the next?

Wednesday, 23 January

Knee swollen like hell. What on earth's the matter with the bloody thing? Even the doctor couldn't understand why it should be up after draining the fluid away. Did some straight-leg lifts again to try to build up the strength, but I reckon I do much better to rest completely. Unfortunately, I'm the only one who thinks that way. To complete a bad day, Bev and Jackie had a flaming row. Jackie has been very ratty lately and got steamed up again over a little misunderstanding about collecting a reporter from the airport to write a feature on Ray and myself. The claws were out good and proper and Jackie ended up saying she was finished with us. Never wanted to speak to us again. That would make life a bit difficult, especially as Ray and I get on so well, and so do Ross and Emma. We'll wait and see what happens.

Friday, 25 January

Laser treatment on the knee last night only made things worse. The injury feels dreadful again today. Went to training feeling really dejected. Only intended to do some leg lifts, but ended up doing half an hour's running. Glad I did. The more I exercised the knee, the better and looser it was. The fluid must have tightened the tendons. At least something good has come out of today. Who knows, I might even manage to play against Fiorentina on Sunday.

Sunday, 27 January: Milan 1 (Hateley), Fiorentina 1

Had the knee drained again. Not too bad. I think it's slowly getting better. If we didn't have a match on Sunday, I think the two weeks' rest would do me the world of good. Against that, I desperately want to play if I can. I owe it to the fans and in any case, time hangs very heavy if you miss a match. It's not like in England where you might have a midweek game to look forward to. The club would have me out there on one leg if they could – just for the nuisance value! It's not a very satisfactory way of going about things – draining my knee every other day, dosing me up with injections, and getting me through the next game. A few niggling pains during the night, but it was in pretty good shape this morning. Pleased to see that the San Siro pitch was heavy. Just the sort of surface I like. It convinced me that the leg would be all right, so I took a chance and declared myself fit. Scored again and found no problem whatever with jumping. We should have won 10–1. After the game, the doctor said I had to go away with the team for a friendly match somewhere deep in the south of Italy. The match isn't until Wednesday, but I gather we're going for a couple of days. Liedholm wants me to go so that's good enough for me.

Monday, 28 January

Had a big argument on the phone with Cardillo. He's insisting that I do some interview with a reporter from the *Gazzetta*, but I told him that Mondays were my free days and I treasured them. The last thing I wanted was to be bothered by the press. Cardillo even had the nerve to phone Ray last night at

Giorgio's restaurant to see if he could get hold of me. As it turned out, we were going to Milan anyway today, so while Bev and my sister went around the shops, I did the interview at the Milan offices. Wasn't too bad after all. Afterwards, I met Bev at the 'Duomo' and we went to buy my Rolex watch at a great shop close to the cathedral where the manager speaks English. Finally opted for a beautiful specimen but couldn't collect it for two days because they had one or two minor adjustments to make. It means I shall have to wait until we get back from the friendly on Thursday, damn it!

Tuesday, 29 January

Arrived at a place called Catanzaro on the 'boot' of Italy. What a hole! Poverty everywhere you look. Beggars on every street corner, kids playing in the dirt with barely a stitch on, and some of the worst housing you could imagine. One hell of a difference from Milan. Felt kind of guilty about spending so much on the Rolex when I saw how these people live. Being up in the north spoils you. I had no idea Italy was as primitive as this still. Can see this will be a long two days. Only four telephone lines out of the hotel and no television in the room. What do they do for fun around here? Saved in the evening by the fans at two Milan supporters' clubs we visited. Surprised to find our people so far away from Milan. They're all football daft in Catanzaro. Don't suppose there's anything else for them to do.

Wednesday, 30 January

Planned to sleep in until 11 a.m. but Franco Bergami put a stop to that by waking me at 9.30 a.m. with the electric shock treatment. Great way to start the day, half-asleep with several hundred volts flying through your right leg! Anyway, after one and a half hours of that, I managed to make it down to the pre-match as they call it. That means signing autographs and posing for pictures for the best part of an hour. Milan are so publicity-conscious it's amazing. Game went pretty well. I didn't play, but froze to death on the bench in an icy wind watching the team win 5–1. 20,000 people turned up to watch! More public relations work after the game. Went to yet another Milan supporters' club about half an hour out of town. Seen enough of them to last me the rest of the year. Roll on tomorrow. Can't wait to get back to Legnano.

Thursday, 31 January

A long day! We left Catanzaro at 9.30 a.m. and got back to Milan at 6 p.m. Arrived home well and truly knackered. Good news when I returned . . . I'd been selected in the team of best players for the half-way stage of the season. My prize was a very nice gold plaque and an eighteen-carat gold ingot.

Phoned Charlie when I got back to the apartment. Doctors in Nottingham say he might have the same disease which killed David Niven. Hope to goodness they're wrong. We won't know for a month. The important thing now is to keep his spirits up because they drop very fast. Just to pile on the agony, Bev started to feel unwell. We thought she might be pregnant, but this time it's not to be, although I fancy the idea of three children before I'm twenty-four. Then, when we've made our little fortune, I shall have plenty of time to devote to them.

Friday, 1 February

Dennis arrived to clear up a few matters so we took the opportunity of going to Giorgio's for a good blow-out. Giorgio was impressed with the watch and said he'd always wanted one himself. Had a great time, drinking six or seven bottles of champagne (I lost count). Didn't get back home until 2.30 a.m. but made it okay for training. Didn't overdo it. Had the knee drained again, and this time, instead of trickling, the fluid came spurting out leaving the joint feeling really empty. I'm certain we must have cracked it at last. Later, I went with Ray to see Liedholm's private man. That was quite an experience.

His name is Mario Maggi and, according to Liedholm, he's the best man in the world at his job. After listening to him, I could well believe it. I've met him twice before but I'm still not sure whether he's a doctor, a magician or a faith healer. He's certainly a remarkable character: fifty-one years old and a former foreign legionnaire in Africa, Indo China and Vietnam. He has five bullet holes in him for the privilege.

He told me some of his premonitions and inspirations over the years and both Ray and I were spellbound. Once he phoned Liedholm and warned him not to take a certain flight he was planning that day. Mr Maggi had a feeling that something was wrong. Tragically, the plane crashed, killing everyone on board, but Liedholm had listened to his friend's advice and is still around to tell the tale. Similarly, a player at Milan called Andrea Manza was advised by Maggi not to travel by train to his holiday destination. Manza duly took the car instead and the train he would have caught was involved in one of the worst crashes Italy has known.

Is it bullshit, or is this guy psychic? I was trying to figure him out while he talked and he seemed genuine enough. I know Liedholm has some funny superstitions, but if he believes in Mr Maggi, I guess it must be right. Our friend went on to talk about players like Falcao and Rivera who'd come to him in the past with their injuries. After a meeting with the guru, their problems were instantly solved and each of them was able to play again. Incredible! While he was telling us all this, he was rubbing a special oil into my knee. It was made up of cloves and coffee beans from Cuba! He'd first made me remove the bandage that Dr Monti had put on after draining my knee, then he said that doctors were a complete waste of time. (Must say I'm inclined to agree!) He said I wouldn't need the bandage any more, then he took hold of my leg and said that after a couple of hours of pain, all the problems would disappear. Well, I did have a few pains afterwards, but they grew less and less sharp as the night wore on.

Sunday, 3 February

I take my hat off to Maggi! The leg feels terrific. Perhaps cloves and coffee beans are the answer after all!

Monday, 4 February

The knee stayed down again. Such a relief to be able to sit in a chair with my leg bent in the normal way.

Tuesday, 5 February

Fantastic news today. Bev's expecting another baby. She did the home pregnancy test and it was positive. So far she's perfect and showing no signs of morning sickness. Unusual for her because she was very ill with the first two. It would be interesting to have a child born in Italy who could have dual nationality, but after my experiences with Italian medics, I think we'd be much happier at an English maternity hospital.

Sunday, 10 February: Cremonese 0, Milan 1

Good win. A last-minute penalty by Di Bartolomei gave us the points. He never misses! We must not lose any more games now if we are to finish well in the league. Verona and Inter are going strong at the moment, but the rest of the pack is pretty close together.

Monday, 11 February

Awards dinner at the Principe di Savoia. I nearly didn't have anything to wear. Having called into Valentinos in Milan for my new suit, I discovered that it wouldn't be ready until four o'clock in the afternoon. Waited around then went back home as pleased as punch only to find that the shop had rung to say they'd given me the wrong trousers. Typical! Luckily, they managed to get the right ones to the hotel in time. Nardi and his wife came along to represent the club because Cardillo had been involved in a minor car crash. A great honour for me – I won the award for the best foreign player in Italy . . . and that's saying quite a lot with the likes of Falcao, Rummenigge, Platini and Maradona for competition! I won a gold trophy which is mine to keep.

Tuesday, 12 February

As much as I try to push it to the back of mind, the knee keeps occupying my thoughts. Can't sleep too well, partly because Emma has got into the habit of sleeping with us, and partly because I'm never relaxed because of the injury worries.

Got up at 11.30 a.m. with the blasted knee stiff and sore again. How the hell can I keep playing like this? Perhaps the pain and swelling is all down to my mental state after all. I'm expecting the knee to swell up after every game, and more often than not it does. Must try to remember what Signor Maggi told me about mind over matter. The doctor confirmed my thoughts that the knee was unusually stiff, and after a consultation with Liedholm advised me to miss tonight's friendly and rest for the Juventus game on Sunday. That's good news. I couldn't possibly do myself justice in this frame of mind. Went to see Liedholm's man, Maggi, again. He was a great comfort and assured me that there was nothing seriously wrong with the knee. Listening to him for half an hour works wonders. Must think positively.

Friday, 15 February

The knee feels exceptionally well. The best it's been for a long time, though I think I've said that before somewhere! Went to training intending to take things easy, but finished up doing a full session with the rest of the boys. Much more range of movement and the spring that's been missing since the operation is back with a vengeance. Straight after the session I slapped an ice-pack on the knee. If it's still okay in the morning I'll definitely be fit for the game.

Saturday, 16 February

Knee feels great. Unfortunately, Bev doesn't. She's still got a hacking cough and flu symptoms, but refuses to take anything for it in case of damaging the baby. Managed to persuade her to get something from the doctor to ease the cough. She won't come to the game tomorrow, but Dennis and Giorgio will. Spent the day relaxing at home. This game could be crucial financially for me and my family and I want to make sure I'm at my best. That means 100 per cent mental and physical condition.

7
IT NEVER RAINS . . .

Why is the Juventus game so full of financial potential for me? Dennis believes the time is ripe for me to be marketed as a commercial commodity. We already have this contract with Nike for me to wear their boots, but we think we can improve on that. What's the point of having an agent unless he can negotiate the best possible deals? With the following I've built up in Italy, Dennis thinks the possibilities are enormous.

Sunday, 17 February: Milan 3, Juventus 2

I played well though I didn't get onto the score-sheet. Am playing up front on my own with Virdis withdrawn into midfield. Eighty thousand screaming fans in the San Siro. The atmosphere was electric. Paolo Rossi scored one of their goals. There's a strong rumour about that Milan are trying to line up an exchange deal with Juventus involving Rossi and me. There was an interview on television after the game with their chairman, Agnelli, saying he'd like to have me in his team. What Agnelli wants he usually gets, but I'm not concerning myself with that. All those dealings are in Dennis's hands. He doesn't burden me with them. I wonder if it's coincidence that Agnelli sent me a get-well-soon card after my operation? Other rumours suggest that Rossi is already 'bought' for next season. Farina is a close pal of his since their days together at Vicenza, when Farina owned the club and Rossi played for them. People in the know believe that it's only a matter of time before they're reunited. We'll have to see what happens.

Monday, 18 February

Went with Bev and Dennis and his wife to the World Sports Fair in Milan. Very impressive. Went to the Nike stand and collected some tremendous gear. I spent four hours on the stand signing autographs. The Nike reps seemed well pleased with the attention we were getting. Dennis then took me to the big clothing companies like Ellesse and Benzi Benson. He's trying to arrange a contract for me to model some of their stuff. The talks apparently went well, but as soon as Nike found out what was going on, they offered us another contract to wear their full range of sports clothes as well as the boots. Dennis played it cool and said he'd be back in touch in a few days. Most important thing now is to work out a proper deal with Milan over advertising rights.

At 5 p.m., Dennis went to Via Turrati to see Cardillo. The meeting had been arranged at Milan's request, but quietly because we didn't want the English or Italian press getting hold of it – not yet anyway. The result was a flaming row with Cardillo. Milan were claiming my total advertising rights without any guarantees or fees. Dennis wouldn't accept that and threatened Cardillo with legal action unless a compromise was worked out. The point was that I was contracted to Milan to play football – full stop. Cardillo finally agreed to defer the matter until Dennis could meet Farina in a couple of weeks. While we were on the subject, Dennis brought up the question of my football contract too. He told Cardillo that my value had increased tremendously since joining Milan and that the issue should be reviewed at the meeting with Farina. You should have seen the colour drain from Cardillo's face! They're not used to people standing up to their domineering attitudes.

Dennis Roach:
'Since the original contract was drawn up between Mark and Milan, the player had become an entirely different proposition.

The club had signed an English Second Division footballer, but within a short time, they owned a phenomenon called "Attila" who was in great demand as a personality and as an advertising medium. Milan had just formed a new company called Milan Promotions and obviously Mark was their prime asset. They were already producing promotional items such as scarves, badges, replica kits, and even Union Jack flags, such was Mark's popularity.

Because they were such a powerful club, I was happy to discuss their taking over his advertising rights, but only with the proviso that he would receive a healthy percentage of the action. On top of that, I felt the club had a duty to reward Mark for his success on the field. Farina had already hinted in the newspapers that a large bonus could be coming Mark's way, but as yet he'd seen nothing of it. I preferred to get it down on a contract.

The papers were also full of stories about Farina selling Mark to Juventus for £4m. We knew this was impossible. Milan supporters would never have allowed it, but it did seem a good opportunity to discuss contracts. Cardillo suggested I sent a written set of proposals. I went back to England, did as he'd said, got them translated, and telexed them to Farina for his consideration.'

Wednesday, 20 February

Mario Maggi was at Milanello to see me train today. The knee was quite good although each time I kicked the ball I could feel a twinge which vanished again after a few moments. Maggi pulled me to one side and said that a piece of cartilage left in the knee could have come away at one side. If that's the case, I'll have to have it removed. Phoned Dennis with the news. He said he'd make me a hush-hush appointment with a specialist in England when I flew over on Sunday for the England game against Northern Ireland.

Sunday, 24 February: Roma 0, Milan 1

This win took us to fourth place in the table. One of our best performances of the season. Didn't score, but was quite thankful not to get my leg broken in the last five minutes.

Benetti came charging in on the blind side with a waist-high tackle! Luckily I saw it coming and managed to pull my right leg to one side as we made contact. It was a crazy thing to do and he could have had only one thing on his mind. Even withdrawing the leg, I still received a six-inch gash down the shin. With the England game coming up, it would have been just my luck to get a bad injury, though I don't suppose Mr Benetti was thinking of that. It was plain, vicious thuggery. If the doctors had put stitches in the wound I would have been out of the England game, but they strapped it in a tight gauze bandage to help the skin knit together, so I think I should be okay for Belfast.

Ray and I left Rome the same evening for London to join the England party. I always look forward to seeing the lads again, but it was especially difficult leaving Bev at this time. She isn't feeling well with the baby and hates it when I'm away.

25–26 February

Had treatment on the shin from the England physio and it looks all right. Enjoyed a good evening meal with the lads at the hotel and retired for an early night. Slept with my leg raised to help the swelling to stay down. It worked. Next morning, we trained for a short time before flying to Belfast amid a cloak of security. We stayed at a nice quiet hotel so I don't expect any problems.

Wednesday, 27 February: Northern Ireland 0, England 1 (Hateley)

Scored the second-half goal to bring my England tally to four goals in five games (not counting two substitute appearances of ten minutes each). Not a very pretty match but a great result for our World Cup hopes. Winning at Windsor Park is never easy. Completely different kettle of fish from playing in Brazil. Against Ireland, the ball hardly touched the floor!

When they come to Wembley for the return it should be a football match. Then we can show them how to play properly. Bobby Robson was delighted with the result. In front of that hostile crowd it was doubly good. Some nutters in the terraces threw bottles at John Barnes and Tony Woodcock but the trouble died down pretty quickly.

A nightmare trip back from the ground. First of all we were delayed at Windsor Park because a bomb had gone off near one of the bridges we had to cross, and when we eventually arrived above Luton airport it was fogbound and we had to turn around and land at Manchester. Didn't arrive back at Luton until 4.30 a.m. Dennis met me and I stayed at his house in St Albans.

Thursday, 28 February

Spent the day with Dennis buying a few bits and bobs to take back to Bev. I bought twenty-five pounds of sausages to smuggle back to Italy. The kids love them and after a few days of lasagne, it's good to tuck into some old-fashioned sausage and mash with baked beans. Got back to Legnano in the evening knowing that I'd have to be up with the lark in the morning to prepare for the Naples match on Sunday. It's all go!

Friday, 1 March

Trained in the morning then had a good massage to get Wednesday and Thursday out of my bones. Got back to the apartment to hear that Charlie had been rushed into hospital on a routine check. Not sure what the problem is, but the doctor seems to think it could be a rare disease affecting the blood, muscles, skin and liver. I asked Liedholm if it would be okay to fly back to England after the game on Sunday. He was very understanding and told me not to rush back because there was no game the following Sunday.

Sunday, 3 March: Milan 3, Naples 2

Fortunate win for us but a very useful one. They had a goal disallowed in the last ten minutes. Decided to fly to England tomorrow morning.

Monday, 4 March

Left at 8 a.m. and went straight to see Charlie in the Queens Medical Centre in Nottingham. He looked very down. The doctors have done extensive tests, but the results are better than we feared. They were most worried about the liver which showed signs of heavy drinking.

The phone never stopped ringing at Bev's mum's house. Farina had done the unforgivable and printed Dennis's private telex in the Italian papers. The discussions were supposed to be in the strictest confidence. It was obvious what he was trying to do – depict me as a greedy young rebel to the fans in order to find an excuse to take the offer from Juventus. I wasn't having any of that. For one thing, I wasn't interested in another club. We'd settled down in Milan. I phoned Dennis and he went through the roof.

Dennis Roach:
'I was furious though I shouldn't have been surprised knowing President Farina's reputation. It wasn't so much that the contents were top secret or anything like that – just the principle of the thing. Taking private negotiations to the public through the media was inexcusable. It's simply not done and I wondered whether we could ever trust this man again. In fairness, it appears that the translation, done locally in St Albans, wasn't the best, though Farina's English is almost as good as his Italian, despite his apparent difficulties with the language. We had to assume it was all a device to sell Mark and make £3m profit. The article read as though we were demanding money with menaces, which certainly wasn't the case.

I thought it was very odd that Farina issued his statement through a Turin newspaper. I contacted the *Gazzetta* and their editor agreed to publish a written answer to the accusations. It was vital that I got over to the Milan public that our demands weren't outrageous, as Farina had tried to imply. The *Gazzetta*, and their London reporter, Giancarlo Galavetti, were very good and stuck to their word. The answers were published and wounds started to heal. Farina's lawyer, Roberto Terzaghi, got in touch with me and a fresh round of negotiations was set up.'

The incident provoked a lot of public outcry and upset us needlessly. Although we're happy in Milan, I feel so disgusted with the club I could walk out tomorrow. If they don't come up with the goods soon, I could be on my way. That would show them. Don't see why I should put up with this.

Wednesday, 6 March

Went with Dennis to watch Real Madrid beat Spurs at White Hart Lane. Quite a shock! Later, we went to Tramps night-club for a meal with a few of the players and Rod Stewart. Got back to Dennis's in the early hours, then had a good long lie-in before working out our reply to Farina.

Thursday, 7 March

Busy day. With the help of Giancarlo from the *Gazzetta*, Dennis and I drafted replies to the chairman, and had them translated by a local company to save time. This is what Dennis's letter said:

> Dear President Farina,
>
> I do of course respect your long experience in football and hope that my dealings with Clubs throughout the world over a long time deserve your respect. I greatly value my name and reputation and therefore feel it necessary to reply to your public statement.
>
> As Mark's advisor, I attended a meeting in Milan at your request to discuss two points:
>
> (1) The aim of AC Milan to take total control of Mark's advertising and publicity.
>
> (2) The outstanding problems of his existing contract

which have been going on all season and on which there are still matters outstanding.

In the event you did not attend this meeting but asked Mr Cardillo to represent you.

At the end of the meeting Mr Cardillo asked me to forward to you by telex a proposal which would try and settle all matters and secure Mark's future with Milan. I must emphasise that this telex was sent at the request of Mr Cardillo.

May I ask you to examine this telex once again. My proposal was not just to cancel the existing contract but to replace it with a new one which extended Mark's period of stay in Milan. The proposal also accepted the principal that Milan would have sole control of Mark's publicity and advertising. At no time, Mr President, did the telex demand any increase in salary for Mark nor insist or demand anything – it was only a document to form the basis of a discussion.

You refer in your telex to the sanctity of contracts and I would agree with you. Mark has certainly met all his obligations under his contract with you, it is unfortunate but true that Milan has not honoured all its promises. Since he joined Milan there have been many promises made by Milan with regard to conditions and finance which have still not been met. In spite of this Mark accepted that there may have been internal problems and/or misunderstandings and did not choose to make this public knowledge. It is therefore totally unfair of you to make public statements to the effect that large salary increases are being demanded. Being a model professional, Mark will of course honour his current contract and any suggestion of alteration to this only resulted from your discussions on the advertising rights.

Personally all my efforts throughout the season have been to act as mediator between Mark and Milan to secure Mark's long-term future with the club. In view of your comments, I have offered to withdraw from negotiations, but Mark has insisted that I continue to advise him on his affairs.

If there have been misunderstandings or misinterpretations, Mr President, let us get together to rectify these problems for the sake of Milan and Mark Hateley.

Dennis Roach

Dear President,
Since you found it necessary to go public over my personal affairs, I regretfully feel it necessary to answer your accusations.

Since my arrival in Milan, my contract has been plagued by broken promises and late payments. I would make the following points to you:

(1) I have never at any time made any demands for increases in money on my football-playing contract. Please examine the telex again. There are no demands for money and there never have been.
(2) If indeed you do respect contracts so dramatically, why then have you not adhered to contract conditions agreed for me? This season you have consistently broken promises and I still have outstanding payments which should have been paid by the club last September.
(3) At your request I attended a meeting with Mr Roach in Milan at which you were not present. Our discussions with Mr Cardillo were not on any changes in my football contract but on your attempt to take over completely my publicity and advertising in Italy without my permission. Since there was no agreement, Mr Cardillo asked Mr Roach to forward a proposal by telex for further discussion.

    It was my idea to extend my playing contract by one year to settle my future with AC Milan and kill off rumours and speculation of a possible transfer to Juventus.
(4) During my period with AC Milan and the constant problems of late payments I have never allowed this to affect my playing performance for AC Milan, on which you will surely agree. In addition Mr Roach has always insisted that we behave in a professional manner and maintain our contract and he has written

personal letters to you asking for these problems to be resolved.

I would repeat, Mr President, that neither myself nor Mr Roach has made any demands for financial improvements to my playing contract. The proposal submitted was for your consideration which would have enabled Milan to take over my advertising and to have settled my future with the club.

If you re-read the telex, you'll see that at no time is there a request for more money as suggested in the press.

Mr President, every week I give 100 per cent of myself for the glory of Milan. I love and respect the club, the fans and supporters and I had hoped to give everything for the President of AC Milan. The answer is in your hands.

Mark

In the afternoon, having got that off our chests, I went to the old ATV studios at Elstree to interview a prospective nanny. (Her father runs the special effects department.) The girl's name is Clare and she seems ideal. We had a chat and a meal with her father before I drove her up to Nottingham to meet Bev. They took to each other immediately and both girls seemed to like Clare, which is unusual for them at the first meeting. Great if we can tie something up quickly so that the strain on Bev is reduced and she can come out with me more in Italy. After a long chat, we agreed to get in touch during the week to discuss a salary.

Saturday, 9 March

Flew back to Milan where Giorgio, like the true friend he is, was waiting to meet us. He took us straight to his restaurant for dinner and even prepared a veal dish for us to take home to the freezer for tomorrow. Nice thought that there's no game tomorrow. Can have a good long rest before the Inter game next week. Our letters to the *Gazzetta* had the desired effect. Farina tried to come on heavy and proclaimed that he would have no further dealings with Dennis – everything would be handled directly through me. I told him no chance. Either he dealt with Dennis and myself as one unit or not at all.

Dennis:
'Mark was strong enough to stand up to the chairman and that was great news for me. You can only battle for people who give you 100 per cent. Farina saw that we could not be bullied and promptly delegated a lawyer called Terghazi to handle all future business. We set up a system of communication at least, and things started to improve. Let's hope we can clear up the problems once and for all and let bygones be bygones.'

Monday, 11 March

Shopping day. Went out to buy a new television set, a hi-fi system and some wardrobes. To help us with the translations, we collected Giorgio and his wife and hit the streets of Varese. Got a fantastic TV called Saba, but the kids were getting restless so the shopping spree ended early. Fixed up the new set at the apartment and it looks like a cinema compared to the old portable. I managed to find twelve stations, though there should be forty there somewhere. The technician's coming around later in the week to tune it properly. However good he is, don't suppose we'll get 'Coronation Street'!

Tuesday, 12 March

Trained for the first time in a week and expected the rest to have cleared up my knee problems for good. How wrong can you be? Still had the same pains and swelling that I've had all along. Nevertheless, Liedholm kept me there for an extra half an hour's shooting. Both legs felt as if they were dropping off! In the evening, Ray and I did the public relations bit and visited another of the endless Milan supporters' clubs. This was the worst yet – just like a cattle market with people behaving abominably. The Italians are charming people, but when they have to queue up for something they'd trample on their best friend to get there first.

Wednesday, 13 March

Knee still swollen. I'm beginning to wonder if Maggi isn't right and that a piece of the cartilage is floating about inside. Very hard day's work so I wasn't too chuffed when I got home to hear that Bev had arranged for me to open an auction at Giorgio's restaurant. If it had been for anyone else I wouldn't have gone, but Giorgio has helped us so much since we've been here that I couldn't refuse. Tomorrow, the doctor says he's going to drain some fluid off the knee. I'm getting worried again because dad says the swelling can't be normal and could lead to arthritis.

Saturday, 16 March

Took off the bandage the doctor had put around my knee after draining the fluid away and, thankfully, it was as dry as a bone. At least I can face tomorrow's game with some confidence.

Sunday, 17 March: Inter 2, Milan 2

Played up front on my own again. Finding it very difficult competing against five defenders with no support. We should have been two or three up at half-time but let them get away with murder. We're still in there with a good chance of qualifying for Europe and that would be a big bonus for me, financially and professionally.

Bev and the kids left for a few days in Nottingham. So did Ray's family. We'll be joining them after the next match in time for the England-Eire game. In the meantime, it was a strange feeling being in Italy without the two families. Ray and I decided to go to Giorgio's for a meal, only to discover that he and Evonne had gone to England too!

Sunday, 24 March: Milan 0, Torino 1

Key match for us against one of the teams bidding for the title. A bad result which gives Torino the double over us. Brought back memories of when I first injured my knee in Turin before Christmas. It's hell up front on my own and I'm going to be dead lucky to break my recent goal famine with no one to play off. Liedholm had a word with me after the game and said he knew how difficult it was for me. He thought I was doing my job well, but would look at the formation again.

Flew to London straight after the game to meet up with the England team. We rendezvoused at the PFA dinner at the London Hilton. Had a smashing meal and a good chat with a few old friends like Alan Knight, the Portsmouth goalkeeper, and Gary Stevens.

Wednesday, 27 March: England 2 (Stevens, Lineker), Eire 0

We had two new caps starting the game – Gary Lineker and Chris Waddle – with Peter Davenport on the bench. Gary played up front with me and Chris was wide on the left. Considering it was the first time Gary and I had played together, we struck up a fair understanding. The bad part of the evening for me came fifteen minutes from the end when a late tackle from the fullback did both sets of ligaments and strained my Achilles tendon. After the game I travelled back to Nottingham to spend Wednesday with the family. Got a horrible feeling the injury nightmare is about to start all over again.

Thursday, 28 March

A dreadful day. I could hardly walk. Spent the time hobbling around the house in a pitiful state. A long injury could be staring me in the face again. Even a nice quiet meal at a French restaurant in Nottingham couldn't cheer me up.

Friday, 29 March

Back in Italy. Went to Milanello, but with no chance of playing against Avellino on Sunday. The doctor told me the Achilles tendon had a bruise behind it and also that I'd damaged a strip of ligament running up the outside of the ankle. The treatment he prescribed was rest and more rest. He bandaged me up and said not to come back until Tuesday (four days away). That would never happen in England. Treatment would have started immediately and continued all day long until you were fit again.

Thursday, 4 April

First time at the training ground since the doctor bandaged my ankle. It's been two days longer than he recommended, but it doesn't feel right even now. He used a laser on the tendon, but no appreciable difference. Learned today that all players are the guests of Gianni Nardi at a local seafood restaurant. It's his Easter treat. Over the meal I asked him if there was any chance of borrowing one of his flats at Alassio this weekend. He said that would be okay and that he'd be there over the holiday weekend as well. Good bloke, Nardi. About the most decent one there.

Friday, 5 April

Good Friday. Ray and I went to the training ground but the ankle is just as bad as ever. The doctor said the predictable thing . . . rest it over Easter, then we'll check again. I'd have preferred it if he'd said come in over the weekend and have some intensive treatment. Wouldn't mind missing the trip to Alassio if I thought I could get the injury cleared up. He didn't seem to want to know about that. It's the soft option – stick on another bandage and send him on his way!

Tonight, by way of a change, Giorgio took us for a twenty-mile drive north into Switzerland for a Chinese meal! Bev's brother Nick and his girlfriend are with us. We had a terrific meal above the main square in Lugano. It's one of the most expensive towns in the area, set on Lake Lugano and overlooking high mountains. A beautiful spot. Went to the casino afterwards. First time for me. I'm not the gambling sort. Didn't stay long because we had to be up early in the morning.

Saturday, 6 April

Off to the seaside for Easter! Met Nardi on the autostrada to Genoa and made the one-and-a-half-hour journey in convoy to Alassio. Nardi invited us to his own apartment for lunch (eight of us including the kids!) where we met a nice chap called Carlo who's the public relations officer for Alassio. Good bloke to know.

Sunday, 7 April

Easter Sunday. No game today, naturally. The Italian national team is playing Portugal. We had a nice relaxing day on the beach and dined out with Nardi and his friends. He really does look after you. Highlight of the day was the trip in his Ferrari to the restaurant. Now there's a car!

Monday, 8 April

Finished off the Easter break with my first game of golf in two years. Quite pleased with my form.

Tuesday, 9 April

Returned to Milan in a hurry to beat the ever-growing number of cars on the autostrada. Into Milanello for the doctor to take yet another look at the ankle. It still hurts and I get the firm impression that doc has given up on me. Doesn't appear to have a clue what the trouble is, let alone how to treat it. He and I both knew the match on Sunday was out of the question even this early in the week (Tuesday). Poor chap. Felt a bit sorry for him because he must be under so much pressure to get me back in action, yet he's clearly not up to the job. Keeps pumping injections into me, draining the knee, getting out the old laser gun, but nothing works. I bet Farina bawls him out every day that I'm missing. He's onto a money-spinner each time I play, but no 'Attila' means smaller gates and less revenue.

By this time, I must admit I'm wondering if I'll ever play football again. I feel crippled every time I try to walk. Sometimes the pain is so bad I don't know what to do with myself. I'd like to be out of this game for good. There's so much pressure. Pressure to get fit to play; pressure to score when you do play; pressure every time you set foot in Milan and get swamped by supporters. Wouldn't it be pleasant to do a normal job where no one recognised you and it didn't matter if you had a weak knee joint? (It's just me getting depressed because I'm injured.)

Wednesday, 10 April

The doctor actually had me in for treatment all day. Amazing! Water and lasers on the cards today. What the hell's he going to try next?

Sunday, 14 April: Sampdoria 2, Milan 1

Another game missed through injury. That defeat drops us back to sixth place and lessens the chances of qualifying for Europe. Verona, Torino, Sampdoria and Inter are all going strong and you can never write off Juventus. It makes next week's match at home to Verona a vital one for us. Wonder if I'll be fit in time?

Tuesday, 16 April

Emma's birthday. She's four today – the time seems to have flashed by. Had a good day at training. Ran for the first time since the England-Eire match, then soaked my ankle in a bucket of ice before running again. Must keep the upper body fit even if the legs aren't. It would be so easy to fall into bad habits.

Wednesday, 17 April

What a terrible contrast to yesterday. Panic stations as Bev's waters break and the baby starts to come. It's the worst moment in my life. She's only four months' pregnant. My son died at 7.30 a.m. Can't put my feelings into words. People who've been through this sort of thing know the sense of desolation. The fact that it would have been our first boy made matters even worse. Bev was sedated for the rest of the day in hospital. I had nothing better to do but to go training. The ankle didn't hurt today. Somehow it didn't seem important. I must have run non-stop for the best part of an hour and couldn't even remember doing it. Head full of other things. Liedholm sensed something was wrong and took me to one side after training. I told him about the events of the morning. Went to see Bev in the hospital at night. She's terribly upset and wants to come out tomorrow.

Thursday, 18 April

That was easier said than done! You can't take your wife out of hospital without showing your passport. The first I knew about it – they might have told me last night. After they'd sent me half-way around the bloody hospital to pay and then still complained because I hadn't got the right papers, I just blew my top. I went straight back to collect Bev without paying and told them to send the bill to Milan because I'd had enough of their red tape! Most important thing now is to get Bev home and looked after. She's had a terrible experience. Bev's mother arrived in Milan to help look after her.

Friday, 19 April

Trained a little today. I might be able to play against the league leaders in two days' time. It's a miracle! My ankle's nowhere near 100 per cent, but I can put up with the niggling pains. It'll be good to get some match practice. I'm running out of time for the England World Cup qualifier against Rumania. That's one I don't want to miss. Only twelve days to go.

Saturday, 20 April

Prepared for the game as usual by relaxing at home with the family. More important than ever to be home this weekend, though I feel irritable and anxious about tomorrow's game. Bev says I've been like this since I first did my knee back in November. I hadn't even realised!

Sunday, 21 April: Milan 0, Verona 0

Played very well even though I wasn't properly ready. Did the ankle again and had a pain-killing injection to help me through the second half. The pain is so bad that I can only walk through the rest of the match. As if to rub salt in the wound, Farina came into the dressing room after the game and said the ankle wasn't important – only the head. What a twit he is!

Spent Monday sitting in the garden with my ankle stuck in a bowl of ice water.

Tuesday, 23 April

Went for a walk into the centre of Legnano with Bev's mother and Clare, the nanny. Bev rested in the house. It's a surprising village with one very smart clothes shop called Stefanos. Bought Bev a few items as a surprise and, on the way back to the car, stopped to buy her twenty red roses off the market stall. She thought the flowers were lovely but the clothes had to go back!

Wednesday, 24 April

Dennis arrived to see Milan promotions about my advertising rights. Yes, that's still dragging on! I met him at 2 p.m. at Via Turrati. We spent five hours with the solicitor acting on behalf of the club and both sides seemed reasonable happy with the outcome. The chap said he was fairly confident that we could reach agreement along the lines Dennis had proposed, though obviously he'd have to clear it with Farina first. Next morning Dennis hired a car to drive to Turin on other business while I agonised again over the ankle at the training ground. I've played with a few injuries in my career, but this one's a real bastard!

Friday, 26 April

Got the telephone bill – £1,200 for two months. Quite a lot, I guess, but I didn't say anything to Bev. She's still getting over the miscarriage and it's the only way of keeping in touch with her mother. I've resigned myself to missing the England match next week.

Saturday, 27 April

Spent the day sunbathing in the garden. Lovely weather with temperature well up in the sixties. Wished Ray all the best for the match at Atalanta tomorrow and for England on Wednesday. Feel a right heel sitting it out like this.

Sunday, 28 April: Atalanta 1, Milan 0

What a disastrous result. A goal six minutes from time killed us and knocked our chances of making it into Europe. We

Above: Karl-Heinz Rummenigge – lives like a lord in a castle over Lake Como

Below left: Liam Brady loves Italy but jealously guards his privacy

Below right: My escapade with the powerboat champ set a few hearts aflutter

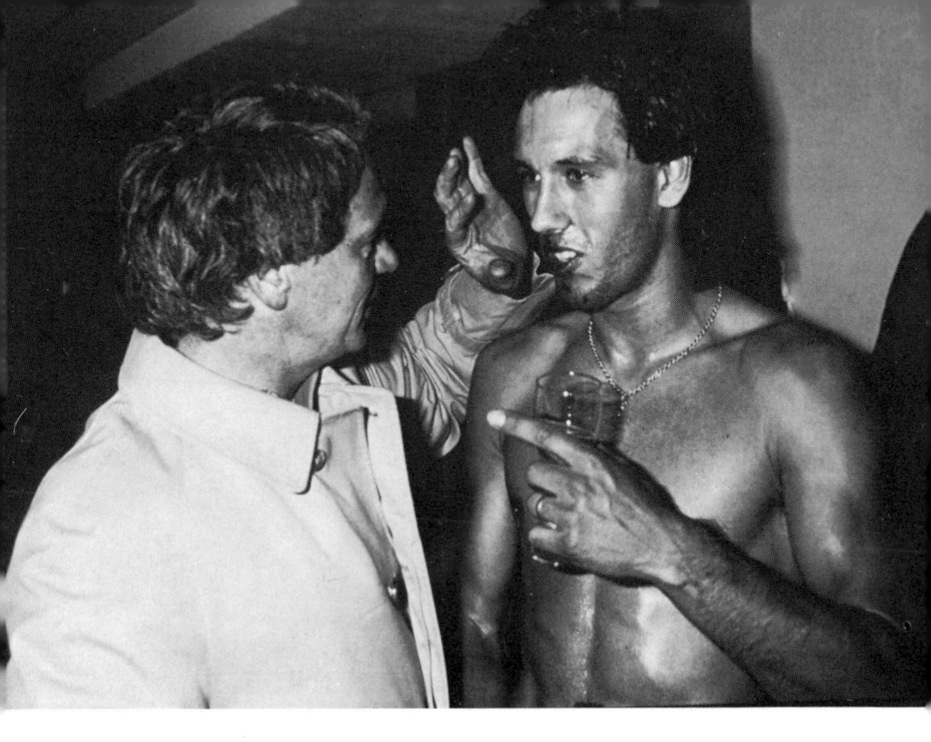

Sympathy from Bobby Robson after taking it in the mouth during the 1984 UEFA Under-21 final

Shattered but happy – Bryan Robson and I wind down after beating Brazil

England v Russia. My instructions were to put the fear of God into them

Second goal against Finland in my first appearance at Wembley

Above: Full length for England's only goal against Italy in Mexico

Below left: Mad dogs and Englishmen! Playing the host nation, Mexico, in the midday sun

Below right: Phew! Heat, altitude and smog take their toll in our World Cup rehearsal

were fortunate that some of the other top teams also lost today. Took Joan to the airport. Bev seems much better and strong enough to look after herself.

8
END OF TERM FEELING

Monday, 29 April

Popped into Milan to do a spot of shopping. Could spend a fortune here, no trouble. Always seem to gravitate towards Piazza del Duomo (Cathedral Square) and the Vittorio Emmanuele gallery. It's difficult avoiding the Rolex shop on the corner. Wasn't planning to go there, but found myself heading in that direction again. Bought Bev a twenty-two-diamond wedding ring for her birthday. As soon as she saw it, she fell in love with it. Diamonds are like status symbols around here. Success seems to be measured in them. In any case, they're a good investment. I fancy having the dial of my gold watch studded with diamonds some time. We've met a Swiss friend of Giorgio's who makes a million importing and exporting diamonds. He says he might be able to help us out. Hell of a character. Apparently he's been kidnapped a couple of times and held to ransom, so he keeps a very low profile these days.

By the time I came out of the jewellery shop, there were a couple of dozen supporters waiting for autographs. Bev hates it but it's a fact of life, I'm afraid.

Tuesday, 30 April

Training at Linate near the airport today because the rest of the lads were supposed to be flying off to Switzerland for a friendly against Naples straight afterwards. Arrived to find the game had been called off because neither Ray nor I were playing. Without 'the foreigners', it's not such a big draw. Tried to run but the leg still aching. No one knew why, so I had another X-ray for my own peace of mind as much as anything. The pictures showed nothing wrong with the knee, so the pain must still be coming from my ankle.

Wednesday, 1 May

Out comes the needle again. The doctor is stumped over the ankle, so if in doubt, bang in another injection! He's using a chemical called oxinorm – the same stuff he's been shooting into my knee. Hope it's more successful on the ankle, that's all I can say!

England drew 0–0 with Rumania in Bucharest today, but I could only watch it on the television. Very hard, physical game. They're not a bad side so the result was pretty good. We kept another clean sheet. Boy, it's frustrating sitting here watching! I'm playing every ball from the armchair. By the end of the game, I reckon I'm as exhausted as the lads out there! Ray had a good game, particularly in the first half. Thought he tired a bit towards the end. Still, we're unbeaten in the World Cup qualifiers, and haven't conceded a goal yet.

Thursday, 2 May

Bev's birthday. While Emma was at school, Bev and I went to Lugano for the day. Clare stayed at the apartment to look after Lucy, so we were *free*. Nice to get out together and forget all about our worries and problems. Lovely warm day, and we took a stroll around the market square before buying Bev some clothes. She can get into a medium-sized skirt again. That made her feel good – just the boost she needs while she's still getting over the depression stage. Once she'd got the bit between her teeth there was no stopping her! We went into Benetton next to buy skirts and t-shirts for the summer and rounded off the day with a great meal at a new restaurant in town.

Friday, 3 May

Back to reality. My ankle was much better in training. The side the doctor had injected was free of pain, so he said he'd put the needle in the other side tomorrow. Feel like a bloody pin cushion! Joined in full-scale training but soon wished I hadn't. My bad luck's incredible. Someone hit a long through ball and as I turned to collect, I felt a searing pain down my back. Had to come off. Doc couldn't believe it. The right side of my back had gone into spasm. He put me back on the table until the muscles eased and told me to go home and lie in the sun. The more heat I could get on the back the better. The only thing left for me to do now is break my neck!

Dennis phoned to say that the contract from Sica, the football makers, was in the post for me to sign. Another good source of income, just from having my face printed on their products, can't be bad. The new Nike deal's taking shape too, he said, so should be ready to sign that soon.

Saturday, 4 May

Decision day about tomorrow's match. An easy one to take – the back still feels dreadful. Bev had to run me a hot bath before I could walk, so no chance of playing. Doc gave me some painkillers to help me sleep and put an injection in my back. A couple of days' rest should do the trick. Maggi the magician came round at night. He stretched my neck and back and rubbed his famous ointment on the painful spots.

Sunday, 5 May: Milan 2, Ascoli 1

Maggi's done it again! Back feels much more comfortable. Poor match but at least we won. The result keeps us still in with a UEFA chance. Vital that we achieve that.

Monday, 6 May

Always look forward to Mondays. No training, no demands. Went to Giorgio's for a super lunch (where else). Ray strolled in about ten minutes after us. What creatures of habit we are! Called into Standa, the department store in Varese, to buy Emma a bike, and loaded up with drink because the Wilkins family are coming round this afternoon. Lazed around drinking and talking. Everything between Jackie and Bev seems to be okay now.

Tuesday, 7 May

Light training. Treating the ankle very cautiously. It means I'm using my right foot more which is good in some ways. It can only improve with use. Went with Ray to one of the supporters' clubs a couple of miles from the training ground. Farina was there cracking his jokes but he ignored me – I still haven't signed my advertising contract with the club! Only men at these supporters' clubs. I'm amazed how many middle-aged blokes support the Milan club, but you rarely see the women. Every club has its groupies but you don't come into contact with them really. It's not like being a pop star – not pursued by hordes of screaming girls everywhere I go or anything like that. I suppose I've been promoted more like Captain America than a sex symbol.

Wednesday, 8 May

Pouring with rain for two days now. Trained all day, got soaking wet and really enjoyed it. Reminded me of a winter's day in England. We ended up playing a match against a young team from Genoa. They were rubbish but it was a good workout for me. We won 7–0 and I scored 4, but more important, the ankle and the back came through it well. Means nothing to score in matches like that but it doesn't do the confidence any harm.

Went into Milan later to collect Bev's ring which had been altered. Stopped for a pizza, then went out for a proper meal in the evening with Jackie and a couple of other friends. Good to get out together, especially for Bev. She's been a bit down lately. When the weather's bad, she gets stuck in the house with only the kids for company.

Friday, 10 May

Training not compulsory this morning, but I did some nevertheless. Yet another anti-inflammation injection in the sore spot behind the ankle bone. If it works as well as the last ones, I should be fit for Sunday.

Saturday, 11 May

It's worked! The ankle feels fine. Met the great Swedish centre-forward Gunnar Nordhal, who was a legend in Italy. He played for Sweden when Liedholm was around. A giant and a lovely man. He must have been some player – he was leading goal-scorer in the Italian league for four successive seasons. Even at sixty-three he still looked as though he could go out there and teach us a thing or two.

Sunday, 12 May: Milan 2, Lazio 0

I didn't score, but was pleased with my game. Made both goals with nod downs; the first one for Virdis and the second for Battistini. Bev brought Emma to the game and said I played all right. I must have done for her to say so! She's normally pretty critical though she only sees the things that I do – she doesn't notice how the team's playing!

Monday, 13 May

Aftermath of my first game for a while – could hardly move this morning! The legs are as stiff as boards and the ankle has seized up. Only natural, I suppose, after a long lay-off. Put the ankle into a bucket of iced water. By the end of the day I was feeling okay again . . . well enough to have a knock about on the tennis court with Bev. It's nice to see her out in the fresh air enjoying herself. Even better when it's with me. I'll try and practise with her every evening if the back permits.

Tuesday, 14 May

Got two days off this week so Bev and I went into Milan while Clare stayed back with Lucy. Top priority was a new suit for the England trip to Helsinki next week. Bought it at Armanis. They give us a 30 per cent discount because they're the club's designers. Got back in perfect time to collect Emma from school and even had time to call into a back-street coffee shop without getting pestered. Ray came round for a couple of beers in the sun. What a difference this weather makes – and the lighter evenings. Had another game of tennis, then went to bed early because Wednesdays are always hard.

Wednesday, 15 May

Watched the European Cup Winners' cup final between Everton and Rapid Vienna. Everton looked terrific, winning 3–1. They've improved beyond recognition. Wasn't too impressed with Rapid, but still a superb win. Managed to keep up the tennis practice in the evening. Wish I could get a few more first serves in!

Thursday, 16 May

Baking hot day. Had a practice match at Milanello. Turned the ankle during the game and heard an ominous click . . . but it settled down quickly and no swelling afterwards. More tennis with Bev when I got back. This'll keep her in shape! Went to Giorgio's for an evening meal with the Wilkins and a chap called Aldo who's organised the plane tickets for the girls to fly home on Sunday. Amazing how useful Giorgio's restaurant is. You can get fixed up with just about anything there.

Friday, 17 May

Building up for the last championship match of the season. We play Como away and a win could ease us into Europe, depending on what the others do. Training is getting better every day. No reaction from the ankle. Went into Milan with Ray's family in the afternoon. We went to collect some free clothes from a shop owned by a friend of Paolo, the club masseur. We spent about forty minutes selecting some really elegant things. The deal was that we could help ourselves in return for doing a company promotion at a furniture shop just down the road. When we got there, the place was heaving with people who'd been waiting two hours for us. We've seen some things, but this was astonishing. The street was jammed with traffic. Italians just stop their cars wherever they want and no one can get by. Don't enjoy this much, but couldn't complain about the deal. Stayed for about twenty minutes. A big relief to get home!

Saturday, 18 May

Full medical examination – passed completely fit. Good news. I'm a certainty for the last match of the season tomorrow. Said goodbye to Bev and the girls who are going to Nottingham while I'm with the England squad for the Finland

and Scotland games next week. Always sad when you have to leave the family for so long. I miss Bev badly.

Sunday, 19 May: Como 0, Milan 0

Disappointing end to the championship. Ray and I played well, but I was disgusted with the attitude of some of the team. They didn't seem to pull out any stops. It was a red-hot day, but that's no excuse. They're more used to it than we are. I felt the fittest I've been for weeks on end, yet we couldn't go out in style. The draw means that we failed to make it into Europe, although there's still the Italian Cup to come. The league finished like this:

Verona	43 pts
Torino	39 pts
Inter	38 pts
Sampdoria	37 pts
Milan	36 pts
Juventus	36 pts
Roma	34 pts

After such a good start, we should have done better than fifth. My absences didn't help much, but the main problem was that we just couldn't score the goals. I'm not too despondent, though. I think we've got the basis of a good side next season. We're young and, so far, we've got no Italian internationals. I think that should come. Baresi, the central defender, has amazed me. At the start of the season I couldn't understand what all the fuss was about, but towards the end he played so well that I couldn't see anyone getting past him. He must have a good chance of playing in the World Cup next year.

My goal total was seven in eighteen games. Considering most of them came in the first few games, it was a disappointment.

Monday, 20 May

Left for Helsinki. A four-hour flight. This is the start of the gipsy life for a solid month. It's the hardest part of football for me . . . being away from the family and living out of a suitcase. But those are the sacrifices you have to make if you want to be an international. You have to be a good tourist. If you can cope with globetrotting and the homesickness, *and* perform on the pitch as well, the rewards at the end of the day make it all worthwhile. When things get tough, I just tell myself that I'm helping to create a good future for Bev and the girls. How many blokes would give their right arms to play for their country?

It was great to see the boys again, especially after missing the Rumania trip. Everybody was in a good mood and the squad spirit is the best I've known anywhere.

Tuesday, 21 May

Had a good long lie-in. No great pressures on us today. Got up in my own time and had a team lunch. In the afternoon we paid our first visit to the national stadium. It was an absolute disgrace. How they could put that place forward as a venue for crucial World Cup games is beyond me. It was like the north face of the moon. I know the Finnish winters are a bit severe, but surely they can do better than this!

We did separate training stints. I concentrated on shooting and heading with Don Howe, and Chris Woods in goal. Enjoyed it. Stayed for about forty-five minutes then went back to the hotel for a bath and change before dinner. After that it was lights out early before the game tomorrow.

Wednesday, 22 May: Finland 1, England 1

A very hard game on a dreadful pitch. The worst I've ever played on. It was a bad start for us. We went 1–0 down in the first five minutes and from then on it was always an uphill struggle. Things improved after the break and I equalised with a right-footer from a pass by Viv Anderson. Caught it well and was delighted to knock it home with the old right peg for a change! We pounded them for the rest of the match, but just couldn't get the winner. Never mind, a draw's not a bad result here and we're still top of the group table with eight points out of a possible ten. Next stop Scotland.

Thursday, 23 May

Arrived at the Marine Hotel, Troon, in the early hours of the morning after flying west straight after the Finland game. The hotel is on Troon golf course – a smashing place to prepare for the auld enemy! Today was a rest day. A few of the lads played snooker in the afternoon which took us through to dinnertime. After eating, I went up to my room to phone Bev who's been in Nottingham all week. She watched the Finland game on television and was pleased with my efforts, if not the result. Then retired for an early night. In the cooler weather of northern Europe, I seem to sleep much better. Those hot, sticky Italian nights can be uncomfortable.

Friday, 24 May

Had another lie-in. Great. They even brought us breakfast in bed. Had a little stroll around the golf course before training in the afternoon. All the work was geared to tightening up the back four. Can't afford to give away goals in the first five minutes! Trevor Francis and I were instructed to hunt the spaces behind the fullbacks. We then had a five-a-side game for half an hour, went back for dinner, and shot off early to bed.

Saturday, 25 May: Scotland 1, England 0

We had an indifferent first half and were lucky not to be behind at half-time. Second half was a different matter. We played really well and should have had a couple of goals.

Missed our chances, though, and Gough popped up with a headed winner fifteen minutes from time. So they take the Sir Stanley Rouse Cup the first time it's awarded, and we're left kicking ourselves for letting the game slip. Not one of my best performances, but the manager seemed fairly pleased. Flew back to Heathrow in the evening and shared a car drive to Nottingham with Viv Anderson. Although he's been with Arsenal for some time, he hasn't managed to sell his house in Nottingham. That must be a drag.

Sunday, 26 May

Great to be back with the family after a week's absence. Dad even came round and we all went out to the pub in the evening. I'd forgotten how nice it was to sit outside and have a pint of lager. At the back of my mind all the time though was the thought that we had to report for the Mexico trip tomorrow, and that would mean another two weeks away. Rounded off the evening with a Chinese meal. My first for ages . . . and my last I should think! Stand by for the chilli con carne!

9
MEXICAN ADVENTURE

A year (give or take a few days) since his goal in the Maracana stadium excited such passionate interest in Milan, Mark Hateley was heading back to Latin America firmly established as England's first-choice central striker. Bobby Robson was taking his team on a short summer tour to Mexico and the United States as an essential part of the build-up to the 1986 World Cup finals in Mexico. In the lung-squeezing heat and the rarified air of Mexico City, some 7,500 feet above sea level, England would play three matches. Apart from the host nation, the opposition would be West Germany and the current world champions, Italy. Robson would lose his three Italian-based players, Hateley, Wilkins and Francis, after the first couple of games. All three were required by their clubs for the final stages of the Italian Cup. But at least they'd be available for the Italy confrontation – the most searching examination yet of England's World Cup pretentions.

Take away the defeat at Hampden Park and it had been a very good year for Robson. Qualification for Mexico in 1986 was, barring some unforeseen mishap, virtually assured, but was the side equipped to achieve anything beyond a place in the last sixteen? Thirteen goals against Finland and Turkey suggested the manager had at last found a formula for success. While not exactly endorsing that belief, the Mexico tour was to offer further encouragement. It was, of course, overshadowed by one of the blackest days in football history, when thirty-six people were killed and hundreds more injured in Belgium's Heysel stadium, the venue for the European Cup final between Liverpool and Juventus. England left for Mexico with two other recent disasters already etched deeply into the minds of the game's followers all over the world – Bradford and Birmingham. Bradford where, two weeks earlier, on 11 May, more than fifty fans were suffocated or burned alive in a blazing old wooden grandstand, and Birmingham where, on the very same day, Leeds and Birmingham City supporters were involved in some of the worst rioting seen on a British football ground. Again, death was in the air. May 1985 was indeed a grim month. As we shall hear from Hateley, the repercussions followed him to Central America and back to Italy.

In the end, Hateley, Wilkins and Francis were doubly thankful to have taken their skills to the continent. Following the ban on English clubs in European competition, they became the only English players allowed through those lucrative portals.

Tuesday, 28 May

Left Heathrow for Mexico. An eight-hour flight to Miami; three hours' wait there, followed by a further three-hour hop to Mexico City. By the time we arrived we were well and truly shattered, but tried to stay awake until 10.30 p.m. to adjust more quickly to local time. We'll have a full week's acclimatisation before the first game against Italy. I've heard all about the altitude problems, but never experienced them. Should be very interesting, though it does make you wonder why the authorities decided to stage the world's biggest soccer competition in a place like this. There again, England did well in 1970 so I guess it proves that anything's possible.

Wednesday, 29 May

Slept very badly, waking at 5 a.m. because of jet lag. All the players have the same problem. The doctor says it'll take five days to adjust properly, so not to worry. Didn't do any training today. Chris Waddle and I went up to the roof of the hotel for a game of tennis to see if there was as big a respiration problem as we'd been told. Funnily enough, breathing didn't seem too bad, though it was very hot and humid up there. What we did notice was how far the ball flew beyond the baseline, even with the gentlest hit. I suppose a football will behave in exactly the same fashion. We'll soon find out.

I was sharing with Chris because Trevor Francis and I turned out not to be ideal room-mates. We're both strong-willed individuals and frankly didn't hit it off too well. He seemed to think that I, as the younger player, should be running around after him making cups of tea etc. Anyone who knows me could have told him that's not my scene at all. We didn't fall out about it, but I had to insist that we be split up next time.

News came through about the riots at the Heysel stadium. Because Europe is several hours ahead of Mexican time, the details started filtering in around lunchtime. Just can't believe it. We were stunned that people could actually get killed watching the European Cup final. You hear about crazy things happening in South America, but we couldn't begin to imagine how it had happened in Belgium. Never seen the England players so quiet and upset. It immediately struck Ray and me that things could be tricky for us back in Italy. Not only for us, but for Jackie and Bev who would be returning to Milan a few days in advance.

Later on, we watched it all on television in the hotel lounge. Mexican television showed it over and over again, which I thought was a bit sick. Even though we more or less knew what to expect, it was still an awful shock. Seemed senseless to me that the organisers could have put rival supporters from Juventus and Liverpool together like that. It happened a few years ago with Spurs, so surely they should have learned their lesson. It could never have happened in Italy. The crowds are as excitable there as anywhere in the world, but they'd be terrified to go on the rampage – the police would be hitting them over the head with truncheons and pointing guns at them. In my year in Italy, I haven't seen a scrap of what you could call real trouble. Sure, there are a few drunks, but none of the violence and fighting you get in England.

Thursday, 30 May

Phoned Bev first thing about the trouble in Belgium. She was as disgusted with the animals on the terraces as I was. In fact, she cried all night after watching it live on English television. Now that it's sunk in, we're anxious about it rebounding on us in Italy. Feelings between Italy and England are obviously at an all-time low, which was the last thing Ray, myself and Trevor wanted. The other thing was that Milan is only an hour's drive from Turin where Juventus play. Too close for comfort! Bev had heard terrible stories about British buildings being stoned and flags being burned – even children being stoned on their way to school. It sounded horrifying.

There could be a terrible backlash and we could be right in the firing line. I can look after myself, but you worry about the kids and about possible attacks on the house. If Ray and I suddenly became the target of a hate campaign, we might even have to pack our bags and get out altogether. That would be terrible because we both want to stay in Italy and make it our home. Right now, we feel ashamed to be English. Bev has been pestered all day by reporters, but refused to say anything until she spoke to me. I told her to play it down because the newspapers could make it worse with sensational headlines. We didn't want to be giving anyone in Italy ideas, knowing that everything reported in the English papers would inevitably get back to Italy and would probably be exaggerated beyond recognition.

What Bev was getting in England, I was getting from the Italian reporters in Mexico. The phone never stopped ringing. Milan contacted us with strict instructions to say nothing to the press, except that we were disturbed and upset by what we'd seen.

I don't normally like censorship, but in this case I think the club was absolutely right to put the block on. As the day wore on, the events of Brussels took on a different perspective. Watching the television reports, we saw the Juventus supporter with the gun and the Liverpool lads trying to help Italian supporters who were being crushed. The hatred for English fans seemed to be disappearing as soon as the true facts became clear. Ray and I were astonished about the criminal element in the Juventus crowd. During the Italian season, there'd been no evidence of it whatever.

We trained for the first time today and that helped to take our minds off Brussels. Sweltering heat. None of the lads could believe how long we had to stay out in it. When we started, we were told no longer than forty-five minutes. In fact, we were running around for two hours! The Camino Real Hotel where we're staying, is about two miles square and is reckoned to have thirty-two bars. The boss put no great restrictions on us the first few days and nights. He said we were free to have a couple of drinks and enjoy ourselves within reason. Chris Waddle, Glenn Hoddle, Kenny Sansom and I have found one bar where you can only have a yard of ale – nothing else. We've been nicknamed the Yard Squad because we pop in at lunchtime and do the business. Last night in the hotel disco, a few of the England lads ran up a drinks bill of £500. Easily done at these prices. Ray, who became known as the social secretary, told Bobby Robson that he'd take care of it, but the boss was in good humour and picked up the tab himself. In the present climate, I don't think it does any harm to unwind with a drink or two. We're all big boys now. As the games get nearer, none of us will need telling to ease off.

Friday, 31 May

Trained at the Reforma Club where England stayed in 1970. We're working in the late morning which is one of the hottest times of the day. It's murder out there. Because the air's so thin, 75 degrees feels like a hundred! Despite the heat we trained surprisingly hard again. We finished off with a twelve-minute run. They said it was to test our fitness, but if we're not fit at this stage of the season, we never will be. It didn't go down very well.

In the evening, we were invited back to the Reforma Club for a formal welcome to Mexico and an excellent meal.

Sunday, 2 June

The squad went to watch Italy play Mexico in the Aztec stadium. What a fantastic place! The game was a big let-down, though. The Italians have been here six days longer than us so they're pretty well acclimatised. Both teams were poor by my reckoning and the match ended 1–1. Enzo Bearzot, the Italian manager, is obviously experimenting with some of the younger players. There are plenty of them, particularly from the new league champions Verona. Couldn't single out anyone who had a good game though. Watching that match didn't do our confidence any harm at all.

Monday, 3 June

Trained this morning at the Aztec stadium. We had a full-scale game against the 'possibles'. We won 3–0 and I scored my first goal on Mexican soil. Hope it's a good omen for Thursday when we play Italy. After the match, went back to the hotel and lazed about in the room. Chris and I had our usual hamburger and coke in mid-afternoon, swilled down with ice-cold beer. Lovely. Phoned Bev as I have done each day we've been away. She's in constant touch with Giorgio and Evonne back at Varese and the word is that things are very calm in Italy. People seem to realise that it wasn't a straightforward case of Englishmen waging war against the Italians. That's good news.

One thing we have noticed about Mexico City is the pollution. This must be the filthiest city on earth! I thought the fumes in Milan were bad enough, but there's no escape here, even on the roof. The smog is affecting me more than the altitude problems. There are so many cars here, and because the city's in a valley there are no winds to carry the fumes away. My nose is permanently bunged up, and breathing at night is difficult. You can taste the pollution and feel it grating in your throat. Horrible. I've also come out in facial sores which I never get at home.

Wednesday, 5 June

A little light training at the Reforma Club, then we took it easy for the rest of the day to get into the mood for Italy. Dying for the game. Everyone wants to play against the world champions but it's extra special for us. The Italians are scared to death of me – have been ever since I was sent off in that first match at San Siro. I have a much bigger reputation over there than I ever had playing in England. The way the Italian papers exaggerate has helped build up this terrifying image, and the Italian players swallow it. I know that if the England lads can keep hitting over the crosses, my old mate Collovati and his colleagues will be having kittens in the penalty area. If I don't score myself, I should be able to distract them enough for one of the others to nip in.

As much as I love Italy and the people there, nothing would make me happier than to see them thrashed by England tomorrow. Giorgio wouldn't be too pleased to hear me say that about his beloved country, but he hasn't been kicked to death every Sunday like I have. The only way Italian defenders have been able to stop me is by holding me down and the referees have been fooled into accepting it. They don't believe anyone can jump as high as I can without getting a lift. Well, there'll be no Italian referee to protect them tomorrow and I've a few scores to settle. You might say I'm bursting with frustrated anger.

Thursday, 6 June: Italy 2, England 1 (Hateley)

Slept in until 9 a.m. then had to get up because we needed a good hour and a half to get through the traffic to the stadium for kick-off at 2 p.m. Heard the news that FIFA have banned all English teams playing outside England because of what happened in Brussels. It means that all the clubs back home are banned from Europe, which is very harsh. Teams like Everton will have no chance to prove themselves where it counts. From a personal point of view, I'd be glad to see the back of English clubs if Milan manage to qualify for the UEFA Cup. I think that will go for all continental clubs.

English teams have been such a force in Europe the last few years.

We had a good breakfast before setting off because there'll be no time for a pre-match meal. The crowd in the stadium was very poor. It was so hot that the locals were all huddled in the shade. They're no fools. The shade temperature was 86 degrees, so heaven knows what it was on the pitch! Still, it's the same for both teams.

We got an unnecessary lecture from Bert Millichip before the kick-off. He said the whole world was looking at the England team because of Brussels, and if anyone stepped out of line, his head would roll. He seemed obsessed with the idea that one of us might do something stupid. I thought it was a very strange way to talk to professional footballers. Did Mr Millichip honestly believe that we didn't realise the delicacy of the situation? If there's one thing we didn't need telling it was that. We all knew what the game could be like, and that if we knocked anyone down we made sure we picked them up. Stands to reason. The manager didn't have to spell it out. You can sense what he's thinking anyway. All he said was that today was an important day for English soccer. At least he didn't talk down to us.

The two teams took the field in mixed ranks as a gesture to the world that we were friendly nations. There were no players from Milan in the Italian side, but one or two from Inter I knew quite well, such as Collovati, the central defender. They say we're good friends because we kick shit out of each other every time we meet! It's true. Off the field we get on well, but once the whistle goes we get stuck in like nobody's business. It's the only way we both know how to play. We watch the ball, go for it, and woe betide anyone who gets in the way!

We held them very well in the first half. In fact I felt we were the better team. Bearzot had left some of the established stars like Rossi, Tardelli and Cabrini on the bench, which some people might think was fielding a half-strength team. That's nonsense. All three are world-class players, but age was telling against them. It would be impossible for Italy to put out a weak team. Whichever eleven they settled on would be formidable. We went in at half-time 0–0 and feeling pleased with ourselves. It was a real surprise when Bagni deceived Shilton with a cross-shot which dipped into the far top corner. Shilts was beaten by the speed of the ball through the air. Then we hit them with an equaliser. It was a great little move. Glenn Hoddle did well to get the ball out wide to John Barnes and he knocked in a great cross towards my head. Like Shilts, I was nearly beaten by the flight of the ball. I thought it was coming straight to me, but it ended up flying away in front of me. I threw myself full tilt and fortunately managed to get a firm head on the ball which the keeper could only get his hand to. One-one, and what a great feeling. I couldn't have scripted the move better. At that point I was convinced we could go all the way and win. The Italians weren't causing us any great problems. It was England asking all the questions.

Suddenly the picture changed and I understood what it was all about. The Mexican referee had seemingly decided that England had to lose for the sake of football. He gave Italy victory with the most diabolical penalty decision I've ever seen – and in the last few minutes of the game. Gary Stevens was supposed to have fouled Pietro Vierchowod. The linesman didn't raise a flag but the ref saw something no one else did and there was Altobelli making it 2–1. There was hardly any time for us to hit back, though we were playing so well I still thought we could win. We had a much more valid penalty appeal turned down when Gary Lineker was flattened, but the ref didn't want to know. Right at the death I had a header which he decided was a foul, so there was no chance England could ever win. A disgrace, but the fact was that we outplayed the world champions for long periods and overall had the better of the game. Although the Italians had been in Mexico almost a week longer, we looked fitter and faster. For me, it was a tremendous day, whatever the score. In the last four England games, including the one I missed against Rumania, I've been the only one on the score-sheet. It's a good feeling, especially after a lean time in Italy following the injury. We need other people scoring as well though. It would be nice if Trevor could get in on the act – he hasn't scored for England for two years. I think he's perhaps a better player in Italy at the moment than he is in a white shirt.

As for Italy, well, if they're the world champions, I don't think we've anything to fear. They think they'll do well in the World Cup, so we should feel pretty confident ourselves. I thought the two Verona players, Fanna and Galderisi, were their best performers. I'd never bet against Italy in a World Cup, and if they're going to have the trophy taken from them it'll have to be a very good team which does it. Italian footballers play in a mini World Cup every Sunday. Most of the world's best footballers belong to Italian clubs so the level of technical ability is higher than in any league in Europe, possibly the world right now. Name a top player and he's in Italy: Rummenigge, Platini, Souness, Brady, Zico, Maradona, Boniek. . . . The English league must be the hardest in the world in a physical sense, but I doubt it's the best. I think you have to play in both leagues to appreciate the qualities.

Friday, 7 June

A free day. A few of us left the Camino Real for the Reforma Club where we lazed around the swimming pool. It's more peaceful here. The place was empty in fact, so we've been able to play music as loud as we want. Nice relaxing day. Some of the others went to the races, but it doesn't appeal to me. Never has. In the evening, we met up at 7.30 p.m. to talk over yesterday's game before dinner. We're all agreed that it went very well. The boss says we have no reason to be overawed; that we shouldn't make the mistake of giving other top teams too much respect. I agree. On a personal note, six goals in eleven starts for England is very satisfying.

I have to play entirely differently for my country. At Milan, Liedholm has me concentrating on the penalty area. I play up front, no running back, and saving all my energy for in the box. I'm not expected to move out of that middle channel. When I go back to play for England, it's very difficult to adjust because my game's changed 100 per cent. All the things Milan *don't* want from me, Bobby Robson does! He wants me to be more mobile and chase fullbacks, so I have to revert to the old English game. I don't mind. I think it's one of the most important things for an international to be able to adapt.

It's always different playing for your country and playing for your club. I think that's where a lot of good club players come unstuck. They can't make the switch. They can look world beaters on a Saturday afternoon, but put them in a different formation with ten more supposed world-class players around them, and they can find it impossible. I'm lucky that I've been able to adapt, and lucky that I'm never troubled by nerves. I've seen brilliant players freeze in an international shirt.

The challenge of changing my role to suit England or Milan is an enjoyable one. Each time I switch from one to the other I look forward to it. You know what they say – a change is as good as a rest. It's not a question of whose way is right, Robson's or Liedholm's, it's just about fitting in with the rest of the team and playing in a way which brings out the best in everyone. The ideal footballer should be able to play in any position. We're heading that way with men like Kenny Sansom and Bryan Robson. I like to think I'd make a good centre-half if I wasn't a striker. What I do believe is that Liedholm has brought more out of me than I thought I had. If that helps England in the World Cup, so much the better.

Saturday, 8 June

Just a few sprints today. Nothing too heavy with the Mexico game tomorrow. We needed a little workout because we've done nothing since the Italy game.

Bev has gone back to Milan. Spoke to her before she went to make sure she felt okay about arriving alone. She says things seemed to be fairly quiet now, though when she got back to Legnano and took the kids for a walk in the park, she noticed some anti-British graffiti on the walls. That put the wind up her a bit, but she did the right thing – kept her mouth shut and pretended to be Italian. I packed my bags today because I'm flying back to Italy straight after the game.

Sunday, 9 June: Mexico 1, England 0

Played in the midday sun. Talk about mad dogs and Englishmen! It was 105 degrees on the pitch. The game was very slow and not very entertaining, but we had enough chances to have won 4–1. I missed two headers.

The goal that Boy scored to win the match was an incredible shot. You could give him the ball again in that position and he wouldn't score in a lifetime! Crazy result. It means we've gone three defeats on the trot, but there was no despondency because we've been playing well and creating chances. The soccer writer on the *Daily Mirror* is having a tough time of it. He's written a story about Bobby Robson getting the sack, so no one's talked to him on this trip. Don't know what's happened to the *Mirror*. I used to take it regularly, but not any more. Just to put the record straight – we may have lost the last three games but against Scotland I think we played the best we have for a long time; against Italy we played equally well and lost because the referee seemed to be determined that Italy should win; against Mexico, we slaughtered them without getting the goals.

Ray, Trevor and I flew out of Mexico City at 8 p.m. after wishing the lads all the best for the two remaining games against West Germany and the United States.

Monday, 10 June

Arrived in Milan after a fifteen-and-a-half-hour flight. Good to see the family again. Bev looked beautiful. Jackie was there to meet Ray, and Helen was there to collect Trevor, who still had an hour-and-a-half drive to Genoa.

Got back to hear that I'm banned from the first leg of the Italian Cup quarter-final against Juventus because of that ridiculous booking against Como in the final league match of the season. Bev's misread the message from the club. She thought I'd been fined the equivalent of £80,000 but even Milan aren't *that* mean. It actually works out at £2,000, which is bad enough. They really fling the book at you in Italy. Annoying, considering I did nothing wrong in the first place.

Wednesday, 12 June: Milan 0, Juventus 0 (Coppa Italia, quarter-final, first leg)

Didn't watch the game. I was tired after the Mexico trip and preferred to spend the time quietly at home. Very good result for us because Juventus are the new European champions when all's said and done. Having finished sixth in the Italian First Division, I couldn't see them beating Liverpool in Brussels and doubt that they would have done in any other circumstances.

England 3 (Dixon 2, Lineker), West Germany 0

Mixed feelings, if I'm honest, watching the lads get their first win in Mexico. They're my mates so naturally I'm delighted for them, but when new players come into the team and do well, it puts pressure on you to win your place back. When the journalists write stories about Dixon getting two goals on his debut, you can't help wondering whether you're out of favour. It's wrong to think that way, but you can't help it. I feel I've done well enough over the last year to keep my place and I think most people would agree with me now. Even so you can't help those niggling doubts. Charlie tells me that pressure's a waste of time – there's no need to feel any. He's right. I'm making a great living in Italy whatever happens, so England's a bonus. Even if I get into the squad next time but don't make the team, that's still a great honour. You have to think big in this game or you're beaten. If we listened to everything people say about us we'd go to pieces.

Kerry's a very sharp player and I wish him well. Not everyone would have the composure to score two goals on his debut. I think he'd be the first to admit that it was useful to make your international start against a team which had just stepped off the plane. From what I saw and heard, it was an easy game. The West Germans were barely recognisable as one of Europe's best teams. The next England match in Los Angeles should be a gentle stroll for Dixon too. I've not had an easy match since playing for England. It was my bad fortune to miss Turkey and West Germany, not to mention the United States.

Saturday, 15 June

No game this weekend so we accepted an invitation from Alberto Petri, world offshore powerboat champion, to spend the weekend at his place in Viareggio on the Mediterranean. He's another contact we've made at Giorgio's restaurant. Bev became very friendly with his wife (who's one of those glamorous model types), and when he offered to pay for the entire family to stay in a hotel for the weekend, it was too grand an opportunity to miss. Alberto's a great chap. He's got homes all over the world, including one in Varese.

His boat had just been overhauled and he was due to test the engine for the first time. Press, television and radio were all milling around when we got to Viareggio. They must have all been tipped off by someone in Alberto's team. I love speed, so when he offered me a spin in the boat, I couldn't resist. It was a massive thing, more like an aeroplane than a boat. We hit 110 miles an hour. Scared the pants off me! Needless to say, the Italian reporters fanned the flames and managed to make a minor scandal out of a million-pound footballer taking a high-speed jaunt. The club supposedly was annoyed, though I didn't get any direct feedback from them. It was bit like the ski-ing episode. They want to wrap you up in cotton wool but I'm blowed if I'm going to be stopped from doing the things I want to do in my leisure time. They may have paid a million for me, but they don't own my soul!

I drove down to the coast at about 110 miles an hour as well and the police stopped me. Luckily I got off, though they could have had me for not carrying identification papers as well. All in all it was a superb weekend. Thanked Alberto for his generosity. He and his wife are a lovely couple.

Sunday, 16 June: England 5 (Lineker 2, Dixon 2, Robson), USA 0

Another easy game I had to miss. As it turned out, being ruled out of the first cup match for Milan I could have stayed with the England squad. Milan wouldn't hear of it so had to sit at home and suffer. Saw the match on television and it looked a real farce. Like playing a Third Division side. Nevertheless, I must congratulate Kerry and Gary Lineker on keeping up their scoring record. Even against the lesser teams, you've got to stick the ball in the net.

Whatever the strength or weakness of the opposition, England finished the summer tour on a high note which should do wonders for our confidence. I'm patriotic so I'll stick my neck out and say that England will win the World Cup. Mind you, Bobby Robson has got to get it dead right otherwise we're dead. We have the quality players, I've no doubts about that after seeing what else is on offer around Europe. The important thing is to settle on a formation and a pattern of play which will see us through. After that, it'll be no good chopping and changing. If the boss pulls it off, I think he'll retire. I've been impressed with him. Basically, he's a genuine and kind-hearted man in a tough world. I just hope he doesn't dismantle what he's already built.

My last eight for Mexico would be Brazil, Argentina, West Germany, Italy, France, England, Scotland and one of the East Europeans (Poland, Russia or Yugoslavia). Once the other nations get acclimatised, I don't think the host nation will be a problem, though historically they usually do well. I hear we're to spend three weeks in the Rocky Mountains of Colorado getting used to altitude training before travelling to Mexico. Trouble is, our group matches are scheduled for Monterrey which is at sea level!

10
EUROPE, HERE WE COME

Eyes down for a place in the UEFA Cup. Several Italian teams have already qualified for Europe so it might be enough for us to reach the final without winning it. We can't bank on that though. The Italian Cup is a strange competition. It actually began way back in August last year, and here we are ten months later still waiting to decide the issue. We did well in some ways to hold Juventus to 0–0 in the home leg, but we'll have to do even better to beat them in Turin. This will be the first time Ray and I will have sampled the feelings of the Juventus crowd after the Brussels disaster. There's been no animosity to speak of in Milan, but in Turin we just don't know.

Wednesday, 19 June: Juventus O, Milan 1 (Virdis)

We did it! Terrific performance and not a hint of trouble on the terraces. I'm over the moon with my own display and relieved not to feel the slightest twinge from the ankle. I'm well pleased with life. The goal came fifteen minutes before half-time from a free kick on the right taken by Ray. I went to the near post and headed it down through the goalkeeper's legs for Pietro to finish it off. The rest of the game was a rearguard action, but with Platini once more failing to impress, we held on. I almost made it 2–0 near the end, but my header stuck in a pool of water six yards out and skidded the wrong side of the post. Typical. The only drawback – I was booked again and will have to miss the first leg of the semi against our arch rivals, Inter.

Daft decision by the referee. In the first half I took no less than four whacks in the face from Brio and never said a word. Finally my patience snapped when the same player grabbed hold of my arm after I turned him near the box and kept pulling until I was almost falling over. There was another defender coming in and with Brio tugging my arm I just couldn't reach the ball so I turned round to say a few words to Mr Brio and that was that! The ref booked me for arguing, but I wasn't arguing with him. I was protesting to Brio who was standing next to the official. Ray stepped in to try to calm things down, but it was no use. It's my fourth booking in Italy. I've been cautioned in England, but who hasn't? At least my conscience is clear and I don't think I'm letting Milan down because I put everything into my game and Liedholm knows it. Some of the other lads don't seem committed to me, not like English players are anyhow. I've only scored once for Milan in the last six months, but there've been no complaints and I'm not unduly worried. Disappointed, yes, but not worried. Without my injury problems, it's reasonable to assume that I might have doubled my tally of seven goals. At any rate, we're in the semi-finals with every prospect of ending the season on the same high note with which we began. If Sampdoria beat Fiorentina in the other semi, which they ought to, we'll qualify for UEFA just by getting to the cup final. Mustn't let it slip now.

Friday, 21 June

Until Sunday the San Siro stadium means just one thing to the folk of Milan . . . Bruce Springstein. The place has been transformed for his concert today. Bev isn't too keen on his material but I like it. Nothing like whizzing down the autostrada in the open-topped Golf with 'Born in the USA' blasting out on all four speakers!

The concert was amazing. Eighty thousand people packed into the stadium and a performance of incredible energy from Springstein. Giorgio and Evonne came with us. Even Bev was converted – you couldn't fail to be in an atmosphere like that. A point worth making here is that despite all the fans, there was no trouble at all. Why is it pop concerts can go ahead peacefully and football matches can't? Goodness knows how they'll get the stadium back into shape for Sunday's cruncher with Inter!

Saturday, 22 June

Goodbye to Clare, the nanny. As we suspected, the attraction of sunbathing proved too strong and Bev, being an old softie, didn't have the heart to make a rigid set of rules for her to work by. Great shame because the kids loved her. Emma cried her heart out when we came to see her off, but it wasn't working, so there's no point prolonging the arrangement. Heard from Dennis that another stupid article has appeared in the *Mirror* about my powerboat escapade and about Milan's bosses allegedly being dissatisfied with my goal famine. Where do they get their stories from? The reporter, who shall be nameless, also dreamed up the idea that I was unpopular with my team-mates. Trouble is that if you fling enough mud some of it sticks.

The club has appealed against my booking at Juventus and was hopeful of avoiding a ban so that I could play against Inter tomorrow. But no joy, so once more I have to sit it out.

Sunday, 23 June: Inter 1, Milan 2

Took Giorgio and Evonne and Bev to watch. We played well though it was difficult for me sitting in the stands as a mere spectator. Felt so helpless. We got the result we wanted though . . . now we've only to draw the return on Wednesday to be in the final.

Monday, 24 June

Television crew arrived from ITV to film a feature on me and the family. They interviewed Giorgio who spoke in his best English about me, the new 'Jesus Christ' to the Milan supporters. Steady on, Giorgio! After filming around the apartment, the crew took shots of Bev and me and the kids wandering around the shops in Varese. It was a typical scene with me pushing Lucy in the pushchair, but the cameras drew attention to us and, as usual, we were submerged in supporters.

Tuesday, 25 June

Eve of the big match and my mind is working overtime. Always feel keyed up before matches and can never really concentrate on much else around me the day before. Never have a shave until after the game – just a silly superstition. The family and Giorgio's family went with ITV to Lake Maggiore. Curiously enough, it's the first time we've been there. Beautiful sunny day as we took the ferry from Leveno to Intra and drove around the west side of the lake to a lovely little town called Stresa. Apparently it's where the BBC filmed their 'Learn to Speak Italian' series. Prince Charles and Princess Diana were here a few weeks ago and said how impressed they were. It's a fabulous spot, but I think I prefer Lake Como. We've been over to Liam's place on the waterfront several times, and there's something extra special about that area. It's certainly the place for speedboats. Rummenigge has a couple and can be seen zooming up and down Como most days of the week. Liam has a boat too, though he doesn't venture out so much. He's been here for five years so he knows the score and protects his privacy more.

Taking the boat over to the islands for lunch, I fancied the idea of a speedboat myself. My problem would be where to keep it, living inland. Lunch on an island overlooking the lake. This is the life! I'm lucky to live in such a beautiful part of the country and enjoy a climate like this. How could anyone be homesick? Bev says that since she came back from

Nottingham she's begun to feel more and more at home here. I'm sure the weather's got something to do with it. She's keen to bring Lucy and Emma up as two Italian girls. I'll go along with that.

Drove back to Milan later in the afternoon and reported to Milanello for preparation for tomorrow's semi-final second leg. The crunch.

Wednesday, 26 June: Inter 1, Milan 1 (Scarnecchia)

We just did enough to reach the Italian Cup final. Inter played some of their best football for weeks with Rummenigge looking very sharp and Brady controlling the play. They should really have had it sown up by half-time, but could only manage a penalty by Brady. I laid on the equaliser for Scarnecchia which assured us of a place in Europe – Sampdoria, we discovered, had beaten Fiorentina. Alberto Petri and his wife came to the game and met us afterwards. Farina was doing his dance of delight. He'd now beaten his great rivals twice in the same season, Bunches of gladioli were brought into the dressing room for the players to give to their wives and we all trooped off for a night out in Milan. ITV filmed the game and the celebrations afterwards. Rumour was rife in the corridors that Paolo Rossi was definitely on his way to Milan for £3m. Haven't heard any official confirmation of that, but if it's true, it's great news. It would be comforting not to have to play alone up front any more. He's one of the world's great strikers so it would be one heck of a boost to have him alongside.

Thursday, 27 June

What a day for Dennis Roach to arrive from England! It's Common Market summit day with Mrs Thatcher in town and every street and hotel in Milan choc-a-bloc. I met him at the airport and we went straight off to lunch with the representatives from Sica, the football manufacturers. We discussed a two-year contract over the meal in Milan. In the evening, Ray and I had to go into the television studios in Milan for our first interview in Italian. It was part of their preview of the cup final, and what a laugh it turned out to be! We understood most of what they were asking us, but I don't know whether they managed to understand a word *we* were saying. We were sweating like horses in there. It was like a sauna.

Friday, 28 June

It's all go at the moment. Dennis and I were out all morning with Farina's solicitor, Terzaghi, arguing about the advertising contract. I had to leave at midday to get back to Giorgio's and pay Aldo for our air tickets home. Dennis stayed with the solicitor all afternoon and phoned me later in the evening from England to say that he thought we had the basis for an agreement. About bloody time! Milan have dragged their feet over this matter and it has been gnawing away at the back of my mind for months now. Let's hope it's settled at last.

Saturday, 29 June

Bev left for England with the children while I headed for 'ritiro' for the first leg of the final tomorrow. I wouldn't see the family for another week. The next time we'd meet up would be on holiday in Portugal. I'll fly direct from Italy and join them on the Algarve. Gianni Nardi offered us his place at Alassio for nothing for the summer break, but we both feel we must get away from Italy and Italians for a month. There'd be no peace at Alassio unfortunately. Portugal seemed the perfect answer.

Tomorrow will be the biggest day at club level for me since I've been in Italy and I'm very much looking forward to it. Never played in a cup final at club level before, so the new experiences are arriving all the time. Sampdoria are a difficult side to beat with Francis and Souness at their heart, but we have the advantage of the home leg first, which we must win to put pressure on them at Genoa next week.

Sunday, 30 June: Milan 0, Sampdoria 1

Disappointing match and disappointing crowd for a final – only 50,000. We did all the attacking but, true to form, Sampdoria had one attack and Graeme Souness scored after I had hit their crossbar with a shot from the edge of the box. This result makes Wednesday's return extra hard. Somehow, I get the impression that one or two of our players have lost a bit of interest. No names, but not much use looking to them for inspiration in the next leg. In their minds, we've already lost.

Monday, 1 July

Boiling hot day. The thermometer touched 100 degrees in the shade. Had my usual lazy Monday; a good lie-in followed by a game of tennis with Ray and, surprise, surprise, our regular lunchtime trip to Giorgio's. Played another game of tennis with Ray in the afternoon and headed back again to Giorgio's to say cheerio to Evonne's friend Sheila and her little girl, who've been over from England for a few days. We got quite friendly with them and heard her side of a very sad tale. Sheila and her husband, who's a chef at Giorgio's, were separated but stayed together for the sake of the little girl. They'd come over for one last time but it hadn't worked so Sheila was heading back to England for good. Sheila was taking custody of their daughter which greatly upset the husband. What a terrible decision to have to take, and I felt so sorry for the little girl saying goodbye to a father she probably wouldn't see again. Awful! I could never leave my wife and family for anything or anyone. Our happiness is too precious.

Tuesday, 2 July

Phoned Bev four or five times during the day – shows how much I miss her. It's not as if there's something new to talk about each time – just good to hear her voice. Lately the family never seems to be together. I'm being sustained by the thought of us all getting together on Friday for the holiday. Then we can forget football for a whole month. The season in Italy seems to drag on forever.

Set off for Milanello and into 'ritiro' for the last time this season. Thank God for that – I hate it! No pleasure at all being shut away with a bunch of blokes week after week.

Today we were paid for the last time until September. He's a crafty old so-and-so, Farina. Holds onto the cup bonuses for two months so that the interest builds up in *his* bank account, not ours, or so the joke goes.

Wednesday, 3 July: Sampdoria 2, Milan 1 (Coppa Italia final, second leg)

Trevor was missing from the Sampdoria team – he's still recovering from injury – but we were in big trouble when Battistini needlessly gave them a penalty early on. One thing we should have been doing was stopping them scoring! Two-nil down on aggregate became 3–0 in the second half when Vialle scored a second for them on the night. Although we were really up against it, we came back well and Virdis scored to give us a chance. We should have had a penalty when Scarnecchia was chopped down but the ref said he dived. No wonder, with an eight-inch gash down his thigh!

Friday, 5 July

Flew from Linate to Lisbon, then took the local connection to Faro to rejoin the family who left England yesterday. Great sense of relief. In Italy, I'm under the spotlight everywhere I go. Have to prove myself every match. Good to leave it all behind and enjoy some of the benefits money can buy. On the flight to Portugal, had time to think back on my first season on the continent.

It's my own fault, I guess, that it finished on a low note after such a great start. I played too often when I wasn't fit. To play in that environment, you have to be 100 per cent every week, or as near as damn it. That means physically and mentally. In England you can get away with 50–60 per cent, but not here. I see now how stupid it was to rush back from injury.

Having said that, the club was equally stupid to try to get me back into action so soon. They'd have had me standing out there on one leg if they could have – just to intimidate defenders. Not enough thought was given to long-term recovery. It's all about money. If Hateley brings a few hundred thousand more lire through the tills, get him out there! Being new to it all and a bit naive, I went along with it when I should have put my foot down. I was eager to show willing and get back to playing when deep inside I knew damned well that I shouldn't be playing. I've learned my lesson. Don't think I'll be making that mistake again.

Funny thing was I still managed to do the business for England even when the injuries were lurking, which says something about the difference between English and Italian play. Italian defenders had one thing in mind when they played Milan – stop Hateley, or better still, flatten him if you get a chance!

You could argue all day and all night about whether I'd have got my international breakthrough so quickly if I hadn't come abroad. The fact is that I got into the England side before I signed for Milan and played three games on the South American tour. It's also true that when I was having such a good start in the Italian league, I still wasn't the first-choice England centre-forward. Paul Mariner was chosen ahead of me for the East Germany game. It could have been 'out of sight, out of mind' as far as Bobby Robson is concerned, but I prefer to think that he was being loyal to one of his servants. There's no doubt that there's a bit of a mystique about playing on the continent. People back home hear about our daring deeds on foreign soil and because they don't see us every week, I suppose we become distant heroes. On the other hand, if you're not scoring goals or playing well, they'll never hear about you and you might not exist.

I hear that Gary Lineker was offered £400,000 to play for two years with Bari, the east coast club which has just won promotion to the Italian First Division next season. How he could afford to turn down that sort of money I don't know. I know he's on a good whack at Everton, but surely it can't compare with the Bari offer?

I've had my moments of doubt, of course, especially when the family's split up as much as it is in Italy, but how could I have any real regrets about leaving England for this?

By the time I'm twenty-eight I'll be a millionaire at this rate. That means I can then go back home if I want to and, hopefully, play for one of the big English clubs. Because I'll be financially secure for life, there'll be no pressure on me. I have this dream in the back of my mind that I can go back to Portsmouth one day when they're established in the First Division, live on the south coast again, and relax and enjoy my football in a part of the country that I love. If I hadn't moved to Milan, it was on the cards that I'd have joined one of the big First Division clubs in England. I dare say I'd have been very happy at Everton, Liverpool, Manchester United or Spurs, but you've got to think further than that. I could have played for ten years in England and still not have earned what I could earn in three years in Italy.

Well, I can see the coast of Portugal from the plane so the diary goes away for three weeks. No more playing, thinking or talking about football. All I want to do is put my feet up, have a few beers and relax with Bev and the kids. *Arrivederci Milano*!

11
WAR IS DECLARED

Saturday, 25 July

Back to Nottingham for a few days to recuperate before starting my second season in Italy. Marvellous holiday; sun-bathing, drinking, swimming and never having to sign an autograph! Dad and Ken Simco came round to Charlie and Joan's for a reunion, so we all drifted off to the pub for lunch. Just like old times. In the afternoon, went to look at a house in Mapperley with a couple of acres of ground. They're asking £120,000 but Charlie thinks we might get it for £100,000. We're looking for another place to do up but that didn't seem to be the right one. It's a good arrangement . . . the company buys the house, Charlie and Bev's brother Nick do it up, then we sell. Wondering whether to buy a house to keep as a base in England, but the drawback is that as a non-taxpayer, I'm not permitted to. To put it another way, if I did have a house here, I'd have to pay taxes to the Inland Revenue.

Went gliding in the afternoon out in the Vale of Belvoir with a couple of friends. What an invigorating experience! The silence is deafening.

Tuesday, 30 July

End of the summer break. Now it's back to the slog. Left the house in Nottingham at 6 a.m. for Heathrow with Bev. The kids were fast asleep in bed. Gave them both a kiss without waking them – it's the last I'll see of them for two or three weeks. This part of football is a drag – always away from the kids. Felt depressed driving down the M1, and I know Bev knew exactly what was going on in my mind. Met Dennis at Watford for breakfast. We had a forty-five-minute chat before continuing the journey to Heathrow. Bev and I had the best part of an hour together at the airport before the plane left. I felt upset when the time came to say goodbye. It seemed such a short summer together this time. Got into Milan at 2.30 p.m. where Giorgio was waiting to pick me up. That was a nice surprise and so typical of Giorgio. Went straight to the medical centre for the annual check-up. Everything was okay. We collected Ray and Jackie and Giorgio's wife, Evonne, and drove to Lugano in Switzerland for a Chinese meal. Got back at 12.30 a.m. I was glad to get back because I'd been on the go all day.

Wednesday, 31 July

Day one of the new season. I remember this time last year as if it was yesterday. Shows how quickly my first year has flown by.

It was a completely different set of circumstances then. It was all new and exciting, if a little frightening. I didn't speak a word of the language, didn't know the players, apart from Ray of course (and I didn't know *him* that well), and wasn't sure what was expected of me. This time I'm better prepared – like a schoolkid starting his second year. It was the same old routine. Ray and I reported at Via Turrati with the rest of the players amid a mass of chanting fans. The street was at a standstill so getting through to the Milan offices wasn't easy. Jackie took us in Ray's Mercedes for the first attempt. Disaster. Couldn't move at all, we decided on plan B – drive to the Duca di Milano hotel and take a taxi from there. On the way, we found the club coach parked outside the hotel, and got Antonio to drive us in. More successful this time, but we ended up getting the shirts ripped from our backs running from the coach to the door.

This part of the preparation is nonsense in my view. Screaming fans, blocked streets, cars getting wrecked, people getting injured in the pushing and shoving, and policemen getting more and more exasperated. All for the sake of tradition. They must be mad.

We were introduced to the press and photographers as usual, and I had lots of pictures taken with our new signing, Paolo Rossi. I have it on good authority that his transfer was signed, sealed and delivered last Christmas. It was just a case of seeing out last season with Juventus before re-joining his old buddy, Farina. So the business of the first day continued with the traditional lunch at Al Sasino's restaurant. He's a faithful Milan supporter and puts on a spread for the team every year at this time. After lunch we left for pre-season training at Vipitano. That's up towards the Yugoslav border, which meant a four-and-a-half-hour coach trip. Pretty drive through the mountains, but gruelling by the time it's over. Journey was relieved a little by cards, music and sleep.

First person I met when we reached Vipitano was the man from Nike, a chap called Giorgio. Obviously the telexes from Dennis had got through because Giorgio stood there loaded up with boots, shoes and clothes which were greatly appreciated. The first thing he said was, when could he meet Dennis to discuss the new contract? Good to see how enthusiastic he was. A feather in our cap when we go into the negotiations is that the Italian boot and shoe company, Diadora, have already been in touch and are desperate to tie up a deal with us as well.

After a meal at the hotel, I phoned Bev to say we'd arrived okay, and went to bed early with the prospect of tomorrow lurking around the corner. Wonder what horrors it'll bring? If the training's anything like last year at Brunico, we're in for a few weeks of hell!

Thursday, 1 August

Pleasantly surprised! We've been told that we'll run in the morning and concentrate on ball skills in the afternoon, but today's been quite easy. Brunico was three times as bad as this. Our whole bodies ached and the club masseurs were worked to death at the end of day one. The bad news is that, according to the fitness man, things will get progressively harder after the first three or four days. Thought it would be too good to last! Not many fans around yet, thankfully, but there are ten days to go yet. Plenty of card-playing but at least the hotel's good and the food is excellent. We can eat what we want which suits me down to the ground – and we're allowed to have beer and wine on the table. Very different from England.

2–3 August

First few days have been very similar. Not too difficult. The fans have started arriving though and it's getting very hard to move around the hotel with all the autograph-hunters. It's a pain after a hard day's training, but that's the mentality of Milan supporters. They travel to the ends of the earth just to watch a training session in the pouring rain! We've had a real mixture of weather up here – sun, rain, thunderstorms, and snow on the higher ground about a hundred feet up from us. Had a painful tendon today so the doctor strapped it up. Hope it's not the same old bloody problem again. Injuries I can do without this year!

Monday, 5 August

First day in the mountains. Very steep slopes and not so much woodland as at Brunico. We do a special circuit of running for twenty minutes, then we're allowed to run free for another twenty. You push yourself as hard as you want. Ray and I worked hard, but I noticed some of the others took the easy route and stayed on the flatter ground. The winds up here cut right through you. The rest of the lads had their waterproofs on because of the showers. In England, we'd still be running about in shorts thinking it was quite a nice day! The fans are here in force now. About six thousand of them. All the hotels are full and it's impossible to get to the training ground without running the gauntlet.

Monday, 7 August

That was the end of the mountain work. We got off lightly. Today was tactical stuff, ready for the first game against Parma tomorrow. Can understand most of the instruction and discussions. Surprising how well my Italian has come on even without lessons. The rain has been terrible today. We hear that the autostrada two kilometres away from us has been partially swept away. It could be fun trying to get around there tomorrow! I've never known a club like this for playing friendlies across the other side of the nation. There's only Milan in the whole of Italy which travels such big distances. Parma, for instance, is miles away from here. It'll be four and a half hours on the coach, then the long haul all the way north again. Doesn't seem to make much sense, but it has to be done.

Thursday, 8 August

Arrived in Parma ready for a good rest, never mind a full-scale match! Beautiful part of Italy where the ham, the cheese and the Lambrusco come from – delicious! Good memories of this place – I scored a header last year in a 2–1 victory. We did even better this time, winning 3–0, and I repeated my contribution with a header similar to the one against Inter where I climbed miles above Collovati. A comfortable win on paper, but not for me physically. The Parma defenders kicked lumps out of me. Is this what it's going to be like this season? The tedious drive back to Vipitano was relieved by a few beers and endless games of cards. Fell into bed safe in the knowledge that we could have a long lie-in tomorrow.

Saturday, 11 August

The local against Vipitano. These are the games I hate. No motivation, nothing. Might just as well be playing a school game. Thankfully I only played the first half and scored one of the six goals. The second team replaced us and banged in another eight goals after half-time. A complete farce. You get much more out of a training session than this rubbish. I suppose it's an essential bit of diplomacy though, to thank the people of Vipitano for putting us up – or putting up with us!

Monday, 13 August

Left for San Bernadettina right down on the east coast below Rome. I reckon Nottingham would be quicker! The programme was this: a six-and-a-half-hour coach journey south; play the match; have glass of beer; back on coach for a six-and-a-half-hour journey back to Milan, arriving approximately 5 a.m. Great! You can imagine how the game went. For the record we drew 1–1 and I played up front with Rossi. We dovetailed quite well, I thought, and he scored a very good goal. I took three defenders to the far post and Rossi sneaked past my shoulder on the near post to nod the ball home. Very impressive player. The partnership should work well in theory. My job is to take all the weight up front and pull defenders out of position to release other players. He played up front by himself last week, got kicked all over the park and withdrawn. When I'm with him, it's *me* who gets kicked and he does the 'sniffing'.

I was pleased we signed him because towards the end of last season, I found that playing the lone ranger was not on. When my former striking partner, Pietro Virdis, went through a bad patch earlier in the season, Liedholm pulled him back to play just in front of midfield. It worked well for Pietro but left me hopelessly exposed. I know they *can't* do that with Rossi. It doesn't matter how badly he might be playing, he has to play up front. Fascinating to study his play. He has so much experience that he can economise on his movement and sense the moment to make his runs. For me at the tender age of twenty-three, playing alongside him will be invaluable. There's so much I can learn from him and it can only stand me in good stead for the World Cup. Once or twice I've felt that he's a greedy player – you give him the ball, make the run, but rarely get the return. Still, he seems a nice enough bloke so I'm sure we can hammer out an understanding. It certainly does my spirits good to see him still performing at the highest level after all the knee problems he's had. He's virtually playing with one kneecap!

The referees are a big problem. Both matches have been like pitched battles. It's quite obvious I'm a marked man. Don't mind a bit, in fact it's exactly what I might have expected, but without any protection from the officials, it's like walking into a lion's den naked! The San Bernadettina centre-half had to go off with a five-inch gash in his head because he went and got himself hurt trying to stop me. If that's the way they want to play it, they'll have to suffer the consequences. I've no intention of easing off. As anyone will tell you, my best game is when I'm on the attack. I can play the other way, just drifting around winning a few tackles here and there, but it's not my natural style.

Mind you, there's no great pleasure in knowing that you've got to sort someone out every time you go out there. I can't look forward to matches like that. It's all very well me knocking defenders around, but my main job is scoring goals. If I can't even get into the penalty box without the refs blowing for a foul, I've no chance. Seems I've only got to make a challenge and it's a free kick against me. Something will have to be sorted out otherwise someone is going to get badly hurt.

Tuesday, 14 August

Thank God that match is out of the way! Back in Milan at 5.30 a.m. (we've finished our stint at Vipitano). Bev and the family are coming back today, so we can get back to a normal way of life again. They don't get into Malpensa until early evening so I can have a good sleep-in and get over yesterday's travelling.

Had lunch at Giorgio's with Ray. It's always our first port of call when we've been away for a while because it's become a second home to us. We must have spent a few lire there over the last year but I've still to find a better restaurant anywhere in Italy. On the way back, I called into the shops in Legnano to buy some electric fans for the apartment. It's roasting at the moment – every day the temperatures are in the nineties and our place isn't the best ventilated in the world. That'll be a nice surprise for Bev, to be a little cooler in the house. After the lousy summer in England, she'll find this quite a shock to the system. On the phone, she says she's really looking forward to coming back this time. It's not been easy at her mum's. The weather's so bad that the kids haven't been able to get out to play, and everybody's been getting under each other's feet.

Collected Bev and the girls from the airport. Great to be together again. Had half an hour to play with Emma and Lucy before it was their bedtime. Those moments are very precious.

Sunday, 18 August

What I feared has happened. Played Genoa in the first round of the Coppa Italia, and the centre-half was led off the pitch with blood gushing from his head after another dust-up with me. Damned fool was pushing and pulling me all over the place. They must be on some sort of incentive bonus to nobble Mark Hateley. The clashes are happening for one reason and one reason only, though – the refs don't see what's going on. They must be blind because everyone else in the stadium sees it!

Tuesday, 20 August

The situation with the referees has got so bad that Liedholm called a special press conference to demand an improvement in standards. The boss has suggested that referees get together to hammer out the problem of how to give me proper protection. Everybody listens to him. He's one of the most respected guys in Italian football and he fully sympathises with me even if some others don't. Sampdoria's international defender, Pietro Vierchowod, did a piece in the *Gazzetta* claiming that it was all my fault and I should stop crying wolf. He doesn't know – the only reason my elbows go astray is because I'm subconsciously trying to protect myself from injury. It's the bloke that provokes trouble who wants sitting on, not the guy on the receiving end who might be driven to retaliate. Okay, so far I'm unscathed – but sooner or later some fool is going to get me. If the referees don't take some action, it'll get completely out of control. There's no enjoyment in it for me. Before each game now I'm wondering if this is where I get my leg broken or my face knocked in!

I've never had any complaints about Italian refs before – they've been pretty good on the whole, but they do seem to be very naive when it comes to me. I don't say they're bent, but they do seem to be ganging up on the wrong bloke. Until last season, they'd never seen an English-style centre-forward before. They couldn't believe what they were seeing because Italian centre-forwards don't tackle. You'll never see them challenging for a 50–50 ball in the box, and they wouldn't dream of trying if it was 40–60 in the defender's favour! The officials must have come to the conclusion that I must be fouling when I go on for a ball, and decided to stop me this season. A couple of times the whistle has gone against me when the ball is still being crossed from the wing. Hopeless! I don't deny that I lose my temper – who wouldn't? I can hear Liedholm hollering from the bench: 'Mark, keep calm, keep calm!'

Friday, 23 August

The problems of the new season are getting to me before it really starts! Feeling tired and depressed at the moment and can't snap out of it. Don't know whether I'm disillusioned with Italy or what, but I wake up in the morning without the slightest desire to go to work. Not so bad when I'm actually training, but sitting at home I start to mope and get irritable. Don't need Bev to tell me – I'm fully aware of it myself. That feeling of optimism has gone. Such a difference from this time last year! I'm thinking of England more and more, wondering whether we did the right thing selling up in Hayling Island and leaving all our friends. Funny the things you miss when you get homesick: a pint of lager in an English pub; fish and chips; morning papers and television; green fields and that touch of sharpness in the air when autumn comes. Got to pull myself together. Trying to look ahead to the season proper in the next couple of weeks and the England game with Rumania coming up in September. Hopefully I'll start picking up and enjoying my football again.

Saturday, 24 August

Red-hot day – nearly 100 degrees. Everything is dried up and Bev's fighting a losing battle trying to keep the plants on the patio refreshed. The kids are in their element though. Emma could pass for an Italian now, she's so brown. I guess you could say the same for me. There were between two and three thousand supporters at the *training* ground today! Absolutely incredible. A few English Second Division clubs wouldn't mind crowds like that on a Saturday afternoon! It's impossible to get onto the playing area. Our practice match was delayed for three-quarters of an hour while they cleared the pitch of fans.

I hear that things aren't so good in England with crowds down everywhere. Can't believe that Liverpool are struggling to fill the ground. It must be very odd not seeing football on television either. It's a bit different over here. One of the television channels has just signed a £650,000 contract with Milan to cover us exclusively in the UEFA Cup. That could be an expensive deal if we go out in the first round! Don't think we will, though. I fancy us to have a good run.

Spirits picked up a little today after scoring two goals in training. All the suspect joints – knees and ankles – feel A1. More good news is that the referees have taken Liedholm's advice and are sending a panel to watch the Cagliari game in Sardinia tomorrow. Just for this one, the boss asked me to take things a little easier.

Bev has been out with Sonia Petri, the wife of Alberto the powerboat champ, and seems to be making a good friend of her. They spend a fair bit of time in Varese. We've also got Karine, one of our friends from Portsmouth, staying with us. Her husband, Jim, arrives tomorrow while I'm away in Sardinia. Looking forward to seeing him again.

Sunday, 25 August: Cagliari 0, Milan 1 (Hateley)

Everyone on their best behaviour with the panel in attendance. The ref was excellent – best we've had so far. Being a good boy isn't my natural game, but it didn't do me any harm for once! Scored with a header in the first five minutes. Cagliari have really come down in the world. In the days of Gigi Riva they were big-time.

Monday, 26 August

Dennis arrives from England to clear up the advertising contracts and work out a final understanding with Milan. First appointment was at Regimila, the Italian headquarters of Nike, about an hour's drive from home. I've been contracted to Nike for four years, but only for peanuts until I signed for Milan. Now they've doubled my money with a bonus for each World Cup qualifying game I play for England. Today we discussed a new deal over three years to include boots and a whole range of sportswear endorsed by me. Nike intend to promote everything from training shoes to shower bags – all carrying the Nike Hateley motif. They only do it with two other sportsmen, John McEnroe and the basketball player, Michael Jordan. Dennis has been discussing a percentage on turnover along with several basic guarantees, and the deal was concluded over a superb lunch.

We've put together one or two good advertising packages now, including a new contract with the *Sun* newspaper. It involves ten columns to cover the whole of next season, including the World Cup. Dennis has stressed that I've got to keep producing it on the field for these deals to be valid. Obviously it's no good my sitting back thinking that someone will come along and pay me a handsome sum for contributing to an article – they won't if I'm not playing well. But as long as the football carries on the way it has, the advertising revenue should keep coming in. Success breeds success, and a sportsman has to make hay while he can. I don't think anyone would begrudge that.

It's an unusual situation for Milan. I think Franco Barese had a few deals going when he was in the last World Cup, but in general they're not used to players having commercial interests. As far as I know, Ray doesn't have an agent. Dennis has pointed out a few home truths to Cardillo, and the club is at last withdrawing its objections and making a serious attempt to negotiate taking over my total rights. At the moment, all I do is work for their club sponsor and support their merchandised products. Dennis gets on well with Terzaghi the lawyer, but negotiations are still very tight and difficult. Bev and I are both hoping it can be sorted out soon. It'll be a weight off our minds.

We'd like to move to Varese if things are cleared up quickly. Legnano's all right, but if we're going to be in Italy for another two years – and who knows, possibly five – we ought to have a home instead of an apartment. When we first arrived, we didn't know anything about the schooling available in the area, neither did we realise that we'd spend most of our leisure time in Varese. It seems a natural progression to move there. We love the town, the shops, the lake, and Giorgio's, of course. As it's turned out, the schools are much better there too. Getting a house in Varese is one of the suggestions Dennis will be putting to the club.

One day, it would be nice to live in the style of Liam Brady and Rummenigge. Lake Como is a fantastic spot – I can just see myself thundering off in the speedboat to collect the shopping in town! Still, both Brady and Rummenigge are in their thirties and I'm still only twenty-three. There's no rush. It's softly, softly for now. I'm still learning the game.

Saturday, 31 August

Karine and Jim return to England today. Had a great week eating and drinking and enjoying the sights. Had a bit of bother taking Dennis back to the airport the other day – the Merc had a puncture and I was late for training. The club was phoning Bev to see where I'd gone and naturally, she got worried as well. Anyway, Dennis made the flight – just – and all's well.

I took a knock on the knee in training so I'm resting for the Coppa Italia game against Arrezzo tomorrow. There's no way I'll be forced to play again when I'm not fully recovered. Feel sorry for Paolo Rossi. He's in plaster after another bad leg injury and won't be ready for at least six weeks. So the plans for the new season have already been torpedoed. A lot of teams have bought new players during the summer – particularly Inter and Juventus who will start favourites for the championship. Between them they've had the pick of players from Verona, whereas Milan have only made one major signing (Rossi), plus three more for the bench. On paper it looks as though the others have grown stronger while we've sold three players and possibly grown weaker. We'll have to wait and see. You can never afford to underestimate Liedholm, so perhaps we'll surprise a few teams yet.

Personally, I must confess that the adrenalin isn't yet there like it was last season. I realise more than ever now that the players are just pawns in Italian football, so that's the way you have to look at it too. It's a job, a business proposition first, and a source of enjoyment only if it succeeds. The fans are behind me just as much as ever, in fact visiting Milan and Varese is almost impossible nowadays because of the adulation. Of course I'm hoping deep down for the explosive start to the season I had last year, but it's asking a lot for history to repeat itself. I'd settle for an injury-free run and twenty goals in the season.

I'm not looking too far into the future, but the very fact that we're proposing to settle down in Varese indicates that we would like the long-term future to be sorted out. That's never easy in Italy because of the erratic way clubs do business. Players move around so fast, it's hard to remember who plays for whom sometimes. If the advertising deals are all tied up to our satisfaction, that should go a long way towards securing the future. The way I feel now, I don't see any logical reason why we shouldn't stay in Italy for another five years. If the body can keep going, why not? Brady and Francis have grown to love the country, and I imagine the longer you're here the less the homesickness bothers you.

Got the English soccer results as usual from Charlie almost as soon as they were announced on the radio in Nottingham. Delighted to see Portsmouth win again and stay at the top of Division Two. The first result I look for though is Nottingham Forest. What on earth's happened to them? They're having a shocking start to the season, which is a big surprise considering the players they've bought. I'm sure my old mate Neil Webb will do a good job for them, though I'm astonished they let Steve Hodge go to Villa.

Sunday, 1 September

Stayed at home while Milan played Arrezzo. Nice lazy day, though the weather has cooled down a lot. People here say it's the end of the summer. If that's right, we can't complain – it's been marvellous. Milan goes back to work after a month away tomorrow, so the old autostrada will be heaving with traffic again.

Monday, 2 September

Didn't find out until I saw the *Gazzetta* this morning that we won 3–1 yesterday after going a goal down. Arrezzo are only a Third Division side, so we'd have wanted shooting to lose that. Ray scored his first goal this season! According to the reports, which I can get the gist of pretty well now, Virdis had a blinder – scored one and laid on the other two. He's having a great run at the moment. On this form, I can see him getting into the Italian World Cup squad. That would be tremendous at twenty-eight, having been rejected by Juventus and a few other clubs along the way.

Lunch at Giorgio's to discuss Alberto's offer for us all to go to Portofino for a couple of days for a spot of powerboating. It would be a bit of a rush after Wednesday's last game in the Coppa Italia, but I fancy it for a bit of a break. Giorgio's keen, but Bev doesn't want to take the kids and is determined that they won't just be left with a babysitter for two days. Apparently, Portofino's one of the choice spots on the Italian Riviera and it would only take an hour and a half to get there.

Undecided on that. After lunch, we went into Milan to get Bev's watch repaired at my favourite Rolex shop. Besieged by autograph-hunters and harassed by a bossy waitress at one of the cafés in the Cathedral Square. I bought a round of drinks at the bar and sat outside with the kids to enjoy the warm sunshine. The waitress started gabbling about the extra charge for sitting at their tables – she was right, I knew, but she was obviously not a football supporter or she'd probably have turned a blind eye.

Back home, got a call in the early evening from one of the Fleet Street soccer writers to say that Bobby Robson had announced the England squad for Rumania a week on Wednesday. Bobby himself called last week to check that everything was all right, so it was no great surprise to learn that I was in the party! He's named twenty-four players which seems a bit excessive. The question they're all asking is whether I'll be named centre-forward or whether Kerry Dixon will get the vote after scoring four goals in his first two internationals on the American trip. I like to think I'm not going back to England to reclaim my international place because I don't consider that I ever lost it. I hope and expect that Bobby will pick the team which did him proud in the earlier World Cup games – in other words, the lads who delivered the goods when it really mattered. I've scored four goals in three World Cup matches, so surely I've proved that I can be counted on when the going gets tough. That's the advantage I have over Dixon and Lineker.

Kerry's been saying that I have it easier than him because he's under the microscope all the time in England. If he believes that, he wants to try playing under this pressure. Italians don't swallow failure. They expect results as a natural right. All right, folks in England may not hear about it if I go a few games for Milan without scoring, but the manager has his finger on the pulse. If I'm off form, he'll soon find out, don't worry!

The *Sun* sent their man today to write the first of my columns. The contest between Dixon and me is an obvious subject, though I was anxious for the readers not to be kidded that there was any aggro between the two of us, because there isn't.

Decided to pull out of the Portofino trip for Bev's sake. It's unfortunate that she can't really join me on these trips because we haven't found another nanny yet. Time for action on that! Bev phoned her mum who put us in touch with an English girl who'd been a nanny in Canada and was looking for another post. Bev spoke to her direct and she seemed overjoyed at the prospect of coming to Italy. We agreed a salary and arranged for her to come out in a week or so. This time, we must understand each other and make sure the relationship works out. In the past, there's been the temptation to think that when we go back to England for international soccer duty or occasional trips home, the nanny is relieved of her duties and can take a holiday. That's not the case. We want someone with us all the time in England as well as Italy.

Wednesday, 4 September: Udinese 1, Milan 0 (Coppa Italia)

Both teams had already qualified for the final stages of the cup, so the game didn't have any real meaning. Liedholm told us this was our last practice match before the league season started and that's the spirit in which it was played. Nevertheless, it doesn't encourage the supporters much. Let's hope we take it a little more seriously on Sunday. We open our league season with a trip to Bari, one of the newly promoted clubs. When they couldn't get Lineker, they splashed out on the Aston Villa pair, Gordon Cowans and Paul Rideout. Since then, Gordon's broken his leg again which is tragic for him. He'll do well to get back after that. It'll be interesting to see how Rideout's getting on – think he's scored a goal or two in pre-season games. I've never been to Bari but Giorgio tells me it's a nice town which suffers from tremendous heat in the summer. Being that much further south, the heat and the poverty increases.

Friday, 6 September

Bobby Robson phoned again to check that I'm fit and ready for Rumania. Get the funny feeling that I might not play. Nothing he said exactly – just a hunch. Hope I'm mistaken.

12
YE OF LITTLE FAITH!

Sunday, 8 September: Bari 0, Milan 1

Had no sleep the night before the game. Freezing cold one minute, sweating the next. My chest was so tight, I sounded like an old steam train trying to breathe! In the morning, had a temperature of 105 degrees but no question of pulling out of the game. It would look bad missing the Milan match and turning out for England a few days later. In any case, Bobby Robson might think twice about selecting me if I'd been forced to pull out. Dragged myself through the game in sizzling temperatures. It was well over 90 degrees in the shade and there wasn't a breath of air. Not quite what the doctor ordered. Peculiar thing – my temperature had dropped half a degree after the match, but I felt like death on a shovel. Had a job staggering to the coach afterwards.

The Bari fans were just like West Ham's – fanatically hostile to the opposition – and in their tiny stadium you were well aware of it. Met Paul Rideout for the first time. He was pretty frustrated because the referees weren't allowing him to play *his* natural game either, and he suffered the double agony of not being able to speak a word of the language. With Gordon Cowans laid up, Paul had no one to confide in, poor chap. He said he was very nervous about his first league match. It was a typical pipe-opener – both sides doing a lot of sizing up. Bari weren't bad. They'd been promoted with Pisa and Lecce although they were already eliminated from the cup. Icardi scored our goal in the second half.

I was glad to get out of that hothouse. Perhaps Gary Lineker was right after all!

Monday, 9 September

All hell let loose when I got home! According to the *Sun* newspaper, I'd collapsed after the match with chronic tonsillitis. The headline was splashed all over the back page and the phone had been ringing all morning. Bev was completely in the dark because I hadn't been able to get through to her from Bari. She was worried, but couldn't understand why, if I was so sick, no one had been in touch. Even Bobby Robson phoned wondering what the devil was going on. I met him at the England hotel in High Wycombe later in the evening and assured him that the story had been grossly exaggerated. After flying to England, I started a course of antibiotics just to clear up any lingering infection I may have collected. Should be all right for Rumania on Wednesday.

Tuesday, 10 September

We only trained for an hour at Bisham Abbey. Felt slightly weaker than usual but well enough to play. This is an important match for me as well as England. With all the talk about Kerry Dixon, I feel I need a good performance to re-stake my claim.

Wednesday, 11 September: England 1, Rumania 1

The boss was disappointed. He'd said he wanted us to make sure of qualifying for the World Cup finals by winning this one. We let him down but at least we didn't lose. That would have been unforgivable. He couldn't hide his feelings, but he rarely gets angry with us. Says we haven't seen the hard side of him yet!

Glen Hoddle did well from Kenny's free kick for the first goal, but we were a bit naive allowing Catamaru to equalise. It would never have been tolerated in Italian football. He's a good player, but we let him run nearly from the half-way line before shooting. Italian defenders would have had him down before he came within forty yards of the goal! Everywhere on the continent, the defender's priority is to protect his goal at all costs. Giving away a free kick that far out is preferable to conceding a goal. Perhaps we'll have to take a leaf out of their book and get meaner.

Had a fairly quiet game, but I wasn't happy with some of the balls I was getting from fullback positions. Gary Stevens insisted on playing everything up the line and on that surface at Wembley, with the dew thick on the ground, there was no hope of catching the ball. Why don't we play it into feet like the Italians do? That way you keep possession, and if you get hit in the back, at least you've won a free kick. Knocking passes into wide-open spaces down the flanks is a complete waste of time against continental sweepers. I know – I have to live with them every Sunday! It's the way Gary's been told to play at Everton, but if you ask me, it won't do at this level.

Thursday, 12 September

Back to Milan in the morning with the thought that it would take something pretty spectacular for us not to reach Mexico now. Nearly but not quite.

Sunday 15 September: Milan 1, Lecce 0

My goal-less spell continues but I'm not too worried. Liedholm says I'm playing better than anyone in the team right now. We're 100 per cent after two games, that's the main thing. I suppose the knockers back in England will see that my name's not on the score-sheet and assume that I'm slipping. That's their problem. I'm not the sort to lie in bed at night worrying about it. I'm enjoying the game again and all the lads are on my side. They've said I should put two fingers up to the press as soon as I score and have nothing more to do with them. As a team, we've stopped cooperating with Italian reporters because they write such garbage.

Pietro Virdis scored the winner for us and that puts us joint top of the league with Juventus. A long, long way to go yet. Worst thing about the match was getting a nasty shoulder injury. I was sandwiched between two defenders trying to go up for a ball. Searing pain through my neck, back and shoulder.

Monday, 16 September

Left for Auxerre in France and the first leg of the UEFA Cup. A new experience for me playing in Europe, and the same goes for most of the Italian lads. It's been six years since Milan qualified. Looking back, Ray's and my first season with the club wasn't too bad, was it? – reaching the Italian Cup final and Europe for the first time since 1979. We've all been paid a tax-free bonus of nearly £10,000 for qualifying, with close on £4,000 a man if we get through this round. Ray's the only member of the team with European experience, so that'll be vital. We took a two-hour drive from Paris after the flight and went to inspect the Auxerre stadium. It's tiny and very enclosed, just like the baseball ground at Derby, with the crowd almost on top of you.

Tuesday, 17 September: Auxerre 3, Milan 1

My shoulder was playing up badly, so I was advised to see the Auxerre club medic. A bit unusual, this chap – he's an acupuncturist! After a thorough examination, he said my second and fifth vertebrae were out. Not immediately serious, but I'd need to have my back clicked into place before playing, and regular massage would be essential if I was to make a full recovery. He told me the problems with my shoulder and neck were all connected with the spine. Because I do so much power heading which involves pulling back the neck and shoulders, the nerves are always tense. That's why I have to sleep with my head turned to the left. The other way is murder. Have to be careful when playing with the kids as well – any sudden movement of the head can send the neck into spasm.

What I needed now was instant relief, and he certainly came up with the goods. He put eighteen needles into my arm and another fifteen into the shoulder. The effect was dramatic. Within a short time, there was a 90 per cent improvement. The doc amazed me by putting a small laser beam into my ear which he said was a pressure point for the spine. There was a burning sensation, but worth it for the relief it brought. He was brilliant – no other word for it. In fact, he's so good that he's been invited to perform his healing in China, and that's like taking coals to Newcastle!

On paper, 3–1 looks a bad scoreline, but it's no worse than losing 1–0. You've still got to score two clear goals at home to go through. Virdis gave us the lead and after they'd equalised, Di Bartolomei went and missed a penalty. He's been relieved of the responsibility now. Virdis will take them, with me next in line! The French scored two late goals to make it look like a drubbing, but it wasn't. I knew we would beat them at home. They were a neat side, but after playing in that little stadium, San Siro would blow their minds.

Another organisational cock-up after the match – not all of it Milan's fault, to be fair. There was a strike by air traffic control at Paris so all the players wanted to drive back across the border tonight. That way, we'd have been home by nine o'clock tomorrow. Rivera disagreed. He thought it would be too tiring – we'd be better getting a good night's sleep and travelling to the airport in the morning. Considering some of the long hauls we've made for practice games in the past, I was surprised at his decision. Lo and behold, next morning at breakfast we discover that Rivera has driven home himself and left us there! Imagine how chuffed we were when the flight was delayed for five hours at Paris and we didn't get back to Milan until ten o'clock in the evening!

Friday, 20 September

Heard about the earthquake in Mexico. Bev was worried to death. Said she didn't want me going there for the World Cup. Apparently, the Camino Real hotel we used on the England trip was still standing. They tell me it's built on top of one of the Aztec pyramids. It's solid as a rock. Funny thing, isn't it, that all the ancient buildings are untouched after centuries of earthquakes?

Sunday, 22 September: Fiorentina 2, Milan 0

What a nightmare week it's been! This was a dreadful result for us. Fiorentina have been doing quite well, but they're nothing to write home about. Apart from the Argentinian, Passarella, they don't have any stars to speak of. We played very badly. I had a few chances. Could have had two or three penalties. One of them was unbelievable: I'm running through the middle when two blokes ambush me; one drags me down from behind, and his mate hits me in the back for good measure. We've all stopped, thinking it's an automatic penalty and the referee plays on!

One thing about Liedholm – he never blows his top however bad things are. Just says '*tranquilo*', and urges us to be patient. He's seen it all before. No point ranting and raving. It'll be interesting to see what happens to him from now on. He was sixty-three last week and the rule in Italy is that once a trainer reaches that age, he can no longer sit in the dug-out. They think it's too stressful and don't want people having heart attacks all over the place. From what I hear, Liedholm will change his title so that he can carry on where he is. He knows all the tricks.

The press have turned against us something rotten. Having conceded five goals in two games, they've concluded that we're all finished. No half measures in Italy! Platini's having a lean time on the score-sheet at the moment and he's been written off. Last season he could do no wrong. That's how fickle they are. They reckon Liedholm should bow out because he's too old; Ray should be dropped because he's got the same problem; and I should get a boot up the backside because I don't score enough. They went through the whole team, slagging each one in turn. If you let that sort of thing get under your skin, you'd soon be a nervous wreck. Mind you, I don't deny that it would be nice to get a goal. They keep on about the eight months since I scored in the league, but they forget that I wasn't even playing for much of that time. In any case, I've been scoring for England in the meantime, so it's not true to say that the goal touch has deserted me.

Thursday, 26 September

Everyone working extra hard in training this week. We have something to prove to the doubters out there.

Bev hasn't been well for a long time now. Violent headaches and tired out all the time. When I come home tired after training, the atmosphere gets a bit tense. Ever since I've known her she's had niggling problems like this. I've told her she needs more greenstuff in her diet. She can't just go on eating pasta and meat. It's a tough job persuading her – she's never been a great lover of vegetables. You don't get so many out here anyway.

Sunday, 29 September: Milan 3 (Hateley 2, Galli), Avellino 0

The perfect answer. My first league goals since February. The team was absolutely bombing. Galli scored in the first half, then Virdis went on a run, cut the ball back, and I had an easy job to sidefoot it in from close range. Seems simple sometimes, while other times scoring can feel like the hardest job in the world. Suddenly everything was okay again. One goal and I'm a bloody hero! Two minutes later, I got another, a header on the near post. No problem. Even through the lean times, I always *think* I'm going to score.

Got home to hear that a nasty piece has appeared in the

Mail on Sunday suggesting that my future in Italy is under threat. They supposedly lifted a line out of one of the Italian papers saying: 'Hateley is no longer Attila . . . perhaps he never was.' Farina's supposed to have been having a go at me and moaning about 'imaginary injuries'.

A good friend who speaks English perfectly went through the sports pages and assured me that the only thing Farina has said is that he's worried about me arguing with referees – nothing else. The president's been out in Botswana trying to sort out his financial problems for the last three weeks so it's nonsense to claim that he's been having a go at me. There's certainly been no rift between us. Reports like that make you angry because people back home believe them. The truth is that Milan and I are in the process of agreeing a new deal which will double my earnings and perhaps more. They want to take over the advertising rights with big guarantees for me and a percentage of the income generated.

Dennis Roach:
Mark will be the first English player to have this sort of deal. The new company, Milan Promotions, will take over all his advertising and endorsements, then it's up to them to sell Mark as hard as they can. It will bring in substantial sums for the club and for the player. As I see it, there's no limit to what could be achieved. Rummenigge, for instance, has been sponsored by Fuji Film and there's absolutely no reason why a similar deal shouldn't be worked out for Mark. It's up to Milan to make the best of it, although I've given them a few ideas, and Mark and I reserve the right of veto. The money has been agreed – all that's left is to clear up one or two clauses. After what's happened in the past, it has to be belt and braces. It doesn't pay to trust them until it's down in black and white.

Wednesday, 2 October: Milan 3 (Virdis 2, Hateley), Auxerre 0

Just as I suspected, the French players panicked when they came up the tunnel. You could see their heads sinking back into their shirts when the noise from 70,000 Italians hit the air. At that moment, I knew we were as good as through to the next round. We were 2–0 up at half-time and as long as we protected that lead, we'd qualified. Had the pleasure of scoring the all-important second goal. Evani went through and should have made sure himself, but the ball hit the keeper twice and broke wide. The cross came over and the old head did the rest. The fans were brilliant. Never stopped chanting my name. I'd have loved the folks back in England to be there. Then they could see for themselves what a lot of rot has been talked and written about my position in Italy.

Even if he felt like it (which I doubt), Farina knows he couldn't afford to attack me too much in the papers. The fans would never stand for it. If it came to a straight choice between the president and me, Farina would be looking for another job! That's not being big-headed – it's a fact. If he has any doubts about that, he should see the fan mail I've been getting. I must have five thousand unanswered letters in my locker. It's impossible to answer them all. When the club passes them onto us each week, my pile's ten times higher than the rest of the team put together. Amazing, but that's the way it is. The letters come from all over the world. Milan's a bit like Manchester United in that respect – they have supporters' clubs everywhere. People have written to me from Australia, Sweden, Russia, Greece, Egypt, Libya, you name it. . . . At the end of the game, a bunch of them demonstrated in front of the press box. Outside the ground, they were pleading with me not to leave the club.

The fantastic thing is that San Siro is full even with ticket prices increased from £15 to £25 for European matches. Farina could put the price up any time he liked and they'd still come. A bit different from England at the moment! Football is the most important thing in their lives here. It doesn't matter how much money they've got as long as there's enough to buy the fortnightly match ticket. The budget is based around it, then they work out what they've got left for rent and food. For some of the workers, that can't be very much after forking out £25 on top of the usual league prices. For the rest, they're big industrialists who put their names down for season tickets for life. The tribune is always heaving with rich businessmen and their wives.

Thursday, 3 October

Good feeling, waking up with three goals safely tucked away in the last two matches. I'm feeling full of confidence and haven't enjoyed my football so much for a long time.

The results of Bev's blood tests came through and her red corpuscles are way down. She didn't get the right treatment after the miscarriage. They've put her on a course of vitamin injections which should get rid of the migraines and the tiredness. Trouble is, I have to give her the injections . . . and not in the arm either!

Sunday, 6 October: Sampdoria 1, Milan 1 (Hateley)

Four goals in eight days. Incredible how they come in a flood when they come. This was one of my best – probably as good as the goal against Inter last season. Virdis went down the line and crossed. I came running in and connected with my head only a yard inside the box. I caught it fantastically. The keeper was standing in the middle of his goal and the ball flew in like a rocket off the post. Bobby Robson had come to see the game, so it was a perfect moment to produce a goal like that. The boss obviously chose this match because he could run his eye over all three Italian-based players before the Turkey game. Unfortunately, Trevor Francis only played one half for Sampdoria. He's having a bad time.

Robson called in at the dressing room before and after the match. He told Ray and me we were both playing against Turkey, which was very nice to hear. Ray's delighted to get back and win his seventy-third cap. There wasn't time for too much chat though. The boss congratulated me on the goal and said he was surprised we didn't win after having so much of the game. He's right. Sampdoria are nothing like the team they were last season.

Graeme Souness is having a nightmare. He's only been getting four-and-a-half out of ten in the markings, but to be honest, I think he's playing in a bad team. He wishes he could join us and we'd love to have him. Our style would suit him down to the ground.

At least there's some consistency about my scoring at the moment. Hope I can keep it up. Dad says that lack of consistency was his big problem – he'd score a two and a three, then go ten games without hitting the net before coming back with another hat-trick or something like that. Much better to score one goal every week. Hat-tricks are a rarity in Italy and more often than not, one goal can win you a point or two.

Tuesday, 8 October

Bev's improving all the time. On Tuesdays I take Emma to school in the morning while Bev goes out with Sonia (the powerboat champion's wife). She's Brazilian and only speaks a smattering of English, so it's good practice for Bev to be speaking Italian all day. This is the arrangement now – the pair of them go off all day somewhere and I see them when I come back from training in the afternoon. Think they've gone shopping in Milan today. It's good for her to get out. Both of us are getting on well with the language. Friends don't mind the mistakes we make, so it gives us the confidence to keep trying. We go quiet when other people come into the conversation, but that'll pass.

Sonia's husband, Alberto, has just bought a farm near to Varese and we're on the lookout for a house there. Ray will possibly join us. Jackie and Bev have been inspecting the international school at Varese. We'd like Emma to go there if we can get fixed up with the accommodation. If Milan decide to renew my football contract at the end of the year, we'll be on our way. Dennis thinks Milan won't wait until my three years are up before wanting to renew – he suspects they'll want to start talking about a roll-over agreement in the New Year. Alberto has a lot of influential friends in the property market, so we should be able to sort out a good deal on a house in Varese.

Sunday, 13 October: Milan 1, Como 0

Our fourth league win. Vialli scored a superb goal, and I thought for a split second I'd kept my scoring sequence going. I beat a defender and bent my shot inside the far post. The rest of the team were already mobbing me before we noticed that the referee had given offside. Terrible decision. Don't think the linesman was flagging.

Monday, 14 October

Flew to England . . . eventually! There was a bomb hoax at Linate airport so the flight which should have left at 9.20 a.m. finally took off at 4.30 p.m. Everyone's very touchy after the hijacking of the Italian ship, *Achille Lauro*. We weren't allowed onto the plane, which was on the runway surrounded by fire engines. Our luggage stayed out there. No one was allowed near it for three hours until we were called to identify our own bags. Bev and the family are already in Nottingham, but I shan't get a chance to visit Charlie and Joan this trip. They're both coming out to Milan after the England game, so we'll get together then.

Tuesday, 15 October

Day before the World Cup qualifier against Turkey. When we played them this time last year, I was just being opened up and missed the eight-goal affair. Light training at Bisham this morning with everyone in terrific spirits. This is what we've been aiming for for two years. I'm delighted for Bobby Robson that we're on the verge of Mexico because he gave up a great job at Ipswich to run the England team. He's not getting over-excited. He said qualification was what we'd come for, and he wanted us to do it in style so the rest of the world could see that we had a squad of players capable of going all the way.

Myself, Tony Woodcock, Glenn Hoddle, and Ray stayed behind to give Shilton some extra shooting practice – it's true what they say about him! He's about to break Gordon Banks's record of seventy-three caps for England in goal, and the way he is I'd be surprised if he didn't go on to double that figure! He got a little more than he bargained for though. We were blasting them in from all angles, and after about ten minutes Shilts said: 'Okay, chaps, that's quite enough, thanks,' and we all headed back to the hotel. I'm rooming with 'Widdley' Waddle now that Gary Stevens of Spurs is out of the squad. Saw him yesterday though, and he looks lean and mean after his injury problems. He'll be back soon, I'm sure.

Dennis came over for a meal last night, and says he's putting the finishing touches to the advertising contract which he wants me to take back to Italy. It runs to twelve pages!

Wednesday, 16 October: England 5 (Lineker 3, Waddle, Robson), Turkey 0

Day started with a light training session, then it was back to the Crest for lunch and a sleep in the afternoon. Never have any problem dropping off before the game, though some of the players prefer to sit and watch television in their rooms.

When I woke up, the boss told us that we were already qualified for the finals because Northern Ireland had managed a shock 1–0 win in Bucharest. Good old Billy Bingham and the boys! That was an astonishing result and gives them a real chance of going to Mexico themselves. Even we couldn't win out there. The Rumanians must be sick after holding us to a draw at Wembley. It means that if Ireland draw against us next month at Wembley, they're through.

Nice relaxed feeling, knowing that you can just go out there and enjoy the game. People seem to think we should thrash the Turks 8–0 again but that's a tall order.

Great atmosphere in Wembley. Only 50,000 or so fans, but they made themselves heard. There was never any doubt about the result after 'Widdley' put us in front early with a fabulous goal. He beats men so easily it isn't true. Tonight was Gary Lineker's night, though. He scored a hat-trick while I didn't get much of a look-in. Felt I played reasonably well, however. I helped to make the third goal for Robbo and had a shot flash just over the bar in the second half. Had to come off near the end with a pulled groin. Very painful.

What troubled me slightly was reading the manager quoted in the papers saying that he would give Kerry Dixon a run out in the team in the next couple of games. He didn't say anything to me about it. If Kerry plays, it means he's planning to drop me. Seemed a funny thing to commit himself to *before* the match.

Considering we were 4–0 up at half-time, the second half was a disappointment and instead of cracking open the champagne, Robson flew off the handle. He was furious at the second-half performance and gave the midfield and defence a real roasting for not getting the ball into the box quickly enough. He warned us that when we played the continentals, it would be no use keeping the ball in midfield for such long periods. He said once we got it stuck in there, we'd never get it back!

The rest of the country was celebrating, but we were being lectured as though we'd failed to qualify! A strange atmosphere, but I could fully understand how the boss felt. He was depressed because the world-beating performance hadn't quite materialised.

I believe we've got a terrific squad of players, but we might have to adapt our style of play against the best teams in the world. For me, it'll be just like playing in Italy.

Bev and I had planned a night out at Tramps with Gary Lineker and his girlfriend, Michelle, but he had to dash off to Thames Television studios. We went to bed early with a couple of biscuits and a glass of warm milk!

13
ON THE BRINK

By December, Hateley's new advertising contract, drawn up with the full approval of the club's lawyer, sat gathering dust on the chairman's desk. It could have been signed and implemented two months earlier. The reason for the delay soon became apparent, although there was no indication before Christmas 1985 that one of the wealthiest clubs in the world was on the verge of collapse.

Farina had ignored the contract because of far more pressing problems. As suspected months before, the millionaire chairman was reportedly in financial difficulties, and looking for an escape route. The chance came when Milan were eliminated from the UEFA Cup at the quarter-final stage. A passage through to the final of the competition would have attracted sufficient revenue for Farina to stave off the immediate threat of bankruptcy to the club. Within hours of that defeat at home to the Belgian side, Waragem, Farina announced his resignation.

It was so sudden that Waragem took the unusual step of telexing Milan when they returned home, regretting the departure of Farina and apologising for having precipitated it!

The players were told at Milanello where Farina put on his bravest face and explained his decision. He told them about the new baby in the family and how he wanted to spend more time at home, but they weren't impressed. Least of all Hateley:

We knew what was going on. I was disgusted with him. Milan had made a fortune in the four years he was chairman, now he had the nerve to tell us he was getting out. All that stuff about time with the family was bunkum. The club was heavily in debt. That's why he'd tried to sell me to Juventus earlier in the year. It was a mystery to me why there seemed to be so many financial crises with a club like Milan.

At the Christmas party, I challenged Farina about my new contract. Told him he'd let me down badly. He said the contract would be signed when I got off the treatment couch and started playing again. Practically accusing me of feigning injury! I could have strangled him. I reminded him of how I'd risked my career last season by playing so soon after the knee injury, just to keep the fans happy. He seemed to have forgotten that. It was a great pleasure taking money off him when he played Santa and gave each member of the team two gold coins!

Milan were up for sale. Farina's vast majority shareholding meant that he owned the club and could offer it to the highest bidder. The newspapers were full of stories that his own personal debts ran into millions of pounds, possibly as much as £15m including allegations that three millions were owed to vice president Nardi. On top of that the club was £2.5m in debt to the taxman. According to a senior official, the tax arrears were the result of 'slipshod administration' rather than any attempt to defraud. We'd seen similar situations in England where Derby County, Wolves, Charlton and Swansea had all been threatened with winding up petitions. But those clubs couldn't command home gates of 80,000! Farina reportedly asked £18m for his shares but it seems that he finally had to settle for less than half of that. Most of the negotiations were conducted from his ranches in Namibia and South Africa, though he was reportedly sighted in London while the crisis was reaching its peak.

The most likely buyer was Silvio Berlusconi, a builder turned entrepreneur in the grand Italian manner. He owned a small town near Milan; an estimated two-thirds of Sardinia; several factories; a newspaper and, not least, two private television channels. Canale Cinque (Channel Five) was the largest independent station in Italy and Berlusconi had big plans for the new French channel he was about to open. The new 'Wogan' if you like was to be none other than Michel Platini. Berlusconi had already made known his scheme to take over AC Milan, offer Juventus £10m for Europe's star footballer, and convert him into a television presenter as well. There were also plans to open a third television station in Spain. Hateley warmed to the idea of the new man, as indeed did the rest of the team.

When a chairman leaves in Italy, it's like a manager going in

English soccer. Over here it's the chairman who buys and sells and decides which players he wants. So Farina's resignation left us all in the air. I knew Liedholm was one of my biggest fans, but *his* future wasn't certain either. It was great news to read that Berlusconi wanted me in his new set up. And if he was to pour in all the money he promised, it could only be good for the likes of Ray Wilkins and me. In the press, Berlusconi said he wanted to make Milan the best team in the world.

The uncertainty dragged on however. Farina was asking too much and the tax bill was mounting. What's more, none of the players had received his wages or his UEFA Cup bonuses for December. There were vague promises about the money appearing in January. The showdown arrived during the weekend of 18 and 19 January, 1986.

Saturday, 18 January

We were in training when the rumours went around that the societa (board) was in emergency session. We hadn't a clue what to expect. We carried on as normal preparing for the important league game against Fiorentina the following day. In the afternoon, we went to the cinema and returned to Milanello in the evening for more training. No one was allowed to use the phones because we were told there could be an important incoming call at any time. Poor old Liedholm was shuffling about with a face as long as the M1! Later that night, our captain, Franco Barese took the call. The board had resigned en bloc, but we were advised to continue as normal and play the next day.

Barese was also told that the club had until Sunday night to pay off the tax, otherwise there'd be a million pound penalty for each extra day that went by. In effect, the club would collapse unless the Sunday deadline was met. The captain said that if the club folded, we'd all get free transfers and go our separate ways. So after all this time, Ray and I were suddenly faced with the prospect of coming home to England to play. The thought shot through my mind that I could be back in Portsmouth colours about five years earlier than I expected! To be honest, I wasn't too worried. Juventus and Torino had both shown interest in me recently, so there wouldn't be much of a problem finding another club. It would probably have had to wait until the end of the season because every Italian Division One team except Fiorentina had its quota of two foreign players.

Sunday, 19 January

It was the morning of the match before we heard the whisper that Berlusconi had rescued Milan at the eleventh hour. Typically Italian dramatics if you ask me, but a relief to hear we were still in business. We went out at San Siro and played some of the best football we've ever played. For the first twenty minutes it was one-touch stuff. Absolutely brilliant. As though we had a point to prove I suppose. Fiorentina were breathing down our necks in fifth place in the table, but they hardly got a kick. We hit the woodwork four times (I hit the post), and won with a Virdis penalty after I'd been chopped down in the box. What a way to celebrate! Although we reckon that the club's still in breach of contract for not paying our wages, I've a feeling it can only be good news from now. To cap it all, Berlusconi made sure that Ray and I would be free to play for England in the friendly against Egypt. And Bobby Robson has already told us that we're in the team.

After all the rumours and stories, things are still up in the air. Apparently this has happened to Milan a few times before and everyone assumes things will be worked out. I sincerely hope so since the team is now playing some of its best football ever and Bev and I are extremely happy in Milan. Emma is settled in her school and Lucy is speaking good Italian. Although things may drag on over the next few weeks, I am now far more confident that my future will be in Italy.